THE PATH TAKEN

A Father and Son Journey to Santiago de Compostela, Along the Camino Frances

H. M. Rodriguez

THE PATH TAKEN: A FATHER AND SON JOURNEY TO
SANTIAGO DE COMPOSTELA, ALONG THE CAMINO FRANCES
Copyright © 2020 by Hector M. Rodriguez

This story is based on true events. In several instances, names have been changed.

All rights reserved. No part of this publication may be reproduced, distributed, or transmitted in any form or by any means, without prior written permission.

ISBN 978-1-7355584-2-4

For Simon

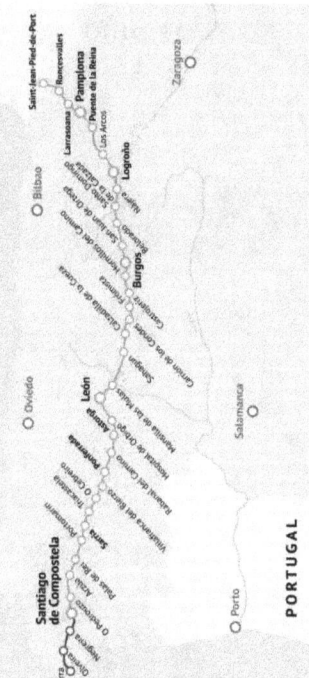

CONTENTS

ACKNOWLEDGMENTS vii
CAPE FINISTERRE 1
RONCESVALLES 15
RUIZ AND PETER 25
CIZUR MENOR 36
ALTO DEL PERDÓN (Mountain of Pardon) 49
AGNES 58
SIMON 64
FATHER IGNACIO AND THE SUNGLASSES 76
TODD AND SILVIA AND BRUNO 85
CRUZ DE FERRO 91
A HIGHER PLACE 100
SANTIAGO DE COMPOSTELA 105
ABOUT THE AUTHOR 111

ACKNOWLEDGMENTS

Thanks to my friends at the Chintimini Senior Center writing group. You guys are so cool. You have endured years of listening to snippets of this story as it came together. During that time, I have had the privilege of getting to know you through your written words. I am truly humbled to have spent this time with you. All I can say is thank you. Thank you for the critical comments, the rewording suggestions, identifying inconsistences, the encouragement, and most importantly, the laughs. It was time well spent and I have learned much! Dr. Johnson, well done.

Carole, Simon, and Mateo, thank you for being my lifeline. You are the anchor to my world. Our journeys continue!

ONE

CAPE FINISTERRE

Finisterre translated from the Spanish means "end of the earth" (*fin* means "end," *la Tierra* means "the Earth"). Cape Finisterre on the northwest coast of Spain was thought to be the end of the earth for thousands of years before we figured out how to build sailing ships and learned that the earth was round. It is the farthest point west a person can travel on the European continent. I thought it would be the end of my *Camino*. My second son Simon and I had just completed the 940-kilometer walk from St. Jean Pied-de-Port in southwest France to Santiago de Compostela, then to Cape Finisterre.

The end of the earth is well-known and significant to Christians for many reasons. James, one of the twelve apostles of Jesus, preached the gospels in this area 2,000 years ago. During his last visitation, Jesus commanded his apostles to go to the ends of the earth to tell everyone about the miracles they witnessed and the truths they heard. James followed this command. He traveled to this area to carry out the will of Jesus. The apostles were not overly successful with their attempts to convert Romans, Basques, and pagans to Christianity 2,000 years ago. But it turns out that James was one of the most successful given that, over the past 1,100 years, so many people from all corners of the world have made the pilgrimage to view his relics.

Close your eyes and imagine no electricity, no smartphones, no lights, no plastic, and no cars. Imagine a time when the only source of heat was fire; imagine a place with only handwoven fabrics for clothing and animal skins for warmth. It was the beginning of the Common Era. People in this traditional setting walked on uneven, unpaved trails, mostly barefoot but sometimes wearing rough, hand-hewn sandals made of leather and wood. Some used donkeys to lighten their loads. Only the wealthy rode horses.

Europe has been inhabited for tens of thousands of years. Archeological discoveries provide evidence of people occupying this region of Spain over 350,000 years ago. One village I encountered along the way was Atapuerca in the province of Burgos. It is set in rolling hills with narrow draws going off to the west. In the draws are caves that contain artifacts of past inhabitants.

I found recorded evidence of someone walking the path as early as 866 AD. Some speculate that the Camino de Santiago was used at least 5,000 years earlier as a trade route. Something attracts people from all over the world to walk the trail. Kings, queens, princesses, princes, warriors, maidens, paupers, peasants, and politicians have made the pilgrimage. Walking the Camino de Santiago changes you. It gives you a gift of awareness that is hard to describe. It helps one find truth and spirit in life. One interesting story tells of how our journey out of Africa millions of years ago followed this path. We have been here before. It gave me a sense of déjà vu.

I met many colorful people along the journey, from all corners of the world. Typically, the travelers or pilgrims are easy acquaintances. You see someone and start a conversation. Your paths may cross again several times. Moving along the Camino, you travel to other places and meet other people. Most travelers are easy to talk with. Most discussions are open and frank. People talk about food, love, politics, religion, blisters, children, and the weather.

This story isn't about any one particular traveler. It's bigger than that. It's about putting one foot down in front of the other and walking through a mysterious and spiritual journey. It's about the people I met and the stories I heard. It's about the experiences on the Camino de Santiago. It's about how a collage of humanity injected hope into my world and helped me understand my spirit. It's about a 56-year-old Boomer embarking on an adventure of exploration, hoping to find more truth in himself and those around him.

In 2014, I was at a holiday party talking with a group of friends. Somehow the subject of the Camino de Santiago came up. Just about every person had heard about it. At some point during our conversations, a spark lit up inside of me. I spoke up: "I should do it. I should walk the Camino. Why not?" This was the decision point that ignited my passion for pursuing the pilgrimage, a journey that would ultimately change my view of the world and everyone around me. Two years later, I walked the Camino de Santiago with Simon, my 15-year-old son.

Another event that roused my interest in trekking the Camino was a movie I saw in 2010 called "The Way." It starred Martin Sheen and his son Emilio Estevez, who wrote and directed it. The movie was loosely based on a few vignettes from the book *Off the Road* by Jack Hitt and featured the adventures, mishaps, starts, stops, paths, roads, trails, hostels or shelters (known as *albergues*), strange people, and comic relief he experienced along his Camino. That is how one references the Camino: your Camino, my Camino, his Camino, her Camino, their Camino.

"The Way" is the story of a father's Camino. The narrator, Tom, is an ophthalmologist living in

Ventura, California. His estranged 37-year-old son Daniel died on the first day of his own Camino, in the high reaches of the Pyrenees Mountains, when he was caught in a sudden change of weather. Tom decides to walk the Camino himself after retrieving Daniel's ashes, hoping to better understand himself and his son.

Tom has a philosophical breakthrough when he remembers driving his son to the airport and lecturing him about life's responsibilities. Tom told Daniel that he made choices. He chose his life and decided on his duties. Daniel disputed Tom's statement, saying that one cannot choose a life; one can only live a life. Daniel represents a free spirit and the passion to explore. The father, Tom, represents the grind of life in which we often trap ourselves. At the end of his Camino, while holding the ashes of his son, Tom finally realizes the truth of Daniel's words.

I studied the Camino extensively for two years before walking it. I read everything I could: books, essays, blogs, and websites. I was amazed at the wealth of historical accounts available. The end of the Camino for most pilgrims is Santiago de Compostela, a labyrinth of ancient terracotta-roofed stone buildings. The road systems in the old parts of the city were designed and built by Romans. Cobblestone lasts a long time when it's done right, and the Romans built infrastructure that survived. Some of the churches date back 900 years; their relics document the spread of Christianity throughout Europe and beyond. The cities, towns, and villages grew and evolved with pilgrims providing a consistent economic flow to the area.

The ancient buildings and churches house vast caverns of artifacts, art, and written accounts of miracles along the Camino. The real teachings of St. James are buried in rich antique archives and stories of people long past. My hope is that this story will find its way into those archives. Perhaps a thousand years from now someone will pick this dusty story off a shelf and try to decipher its contents.

The Camino de Santiago is a personal journey. It is physically challenging, mentally melting, and spiritually refreshing. Simon and I started from our home in Oregon on June 13, 2016, and entered Santiago de Compostela on July 21. We reached many significant milestones together: monuments, markers, and villages. But we did not always walk together. As a matter of fact, we separated after the second day high in the Pyrenees Mountains. We had agreed to meet in Zubiri, a small village in Spain. But I was in too much of a hurry and missed the right-hand turn into the village. I was five kilometers past the turn before I realized I had hiked too far. When I finally contacted Simon, I learned he had met with several older pilgrims on the trail: Jens from Germany, Maggie from Canada, Huy from Houston, and Clinton from southern California. It was a good group of young people whom I grew to respect and trust once I got to know them. They took Simon under their wing that evening, and they all became fast friends. They called themselves the "Shade Brigade" because shade, on some parts of the Camino in July, can be difficult to find.

Simon, my older son, is a good -natured young man. That year he was on the cusp of manhood. Although I invited my wife, Carole, and both of my sons to come with me, he was the only one who showed any interest. I am not sure if it was because he was genuinely interested in coming on the adventure or if he felt that someone needed to watch over Dad. Whatever the reason, I was grateful he came. He took care of me in ways that will resonate for the rest of my life. He gave me memories for this book. I thought it was really cool that he met people from all over the world, and I'm sure the experience will resonate with him as he grows older. He gives me hope that our family's adventurous spirit will survive. I hope the memory will nurture his spiritual heart.

By the time I realized my mistake, it was getting late. I accepted the fact we would be separated for the night, though I worried about my boy. We were in a foreign country, literally thousands of miles from home. We agreed that we would not use phones, so the only way to maintain contact was by email. Most of the establishments along the Camino have Wi-Fi capability as a standard amenity. Simon and I tested the system. We made contact. I told him I had overshot the turn. He told me he met some people from Germany and Canada and they were going to eat dinner together. He said he was okay. The Camino magic was starting to happen. I knew he would be safe. I told Simon I would walk slow in the morning so he could catch up.

While researching the trip, I learned that if you are in reasonable health, the Camino, in and of itself, is safe. Many single people walk the Camino every year. When we were there in July, I met several schoolteachers on summer break. Occasionally you hear of some rogue encounter with a deranged person or someone getting drunk and out of hand, but that type of thing can happen anywhere. Generally, threatening incidents are not common.

After touching base with Simon, I found an albergue in the town of Larrasoaña, Spain, about 20 kilometers from the French border. The Pyrenees Mountains provide a dramatic and intimidating beginning to the Camino. People have written that the Pyrenees prepare you physically for the journey ahead. It is true that once you enter the second stage, the Meseta, you are in better shape than when you started. The Meseta is where you have time to think about people, problems, and pathways that plague you as a person. The third stage of the Camino is about spiritual mending. When I say mending, I mean the suturing of open gaps in one's beliefs. It does not happen all at once, and the answers are often not as bright as you would like them to be. The Camino is notoriously stingy with parsing out meanings and insights. Nevertheless, the Camino is a metaphorical gold mine.

Simon caught up to me the next morning about 10:30. He came up from behind and said, "Hey, Dad." I shed a tear and hugged him hard. He looked good and walked with confidence, a boy on the cusp of becoming a man. His new friends were with him, and I had a chance to watch these kids and look them in the eye. They were good people who were there for a reason, and that reason did not involve backhandedness or malicious intent. As we moved down the trail, they walked ahead of me, and when they stopped, I caught up. They walked faster than I did, plus my feet were developing hotspots, the precursor to blisters. The shoes I bought had not been a good choice, and my feet were getting sore.

As I walked through the Pyrenees Mountains, I saw why it was such a strategic stronghold for Charlemagne, Napoleon, and legions of Romans.

Hundreds of thousands of Basques and Roman soldiers lay buried throughout the deep valleys and thick forests. It would be difficult to run up and down the mountains; even the fittest athletes would struggle to breathe climbing out of the deep river-cut valleys. The Camino trail is probably the easiest route to get through the steep valleys and jagged mountaintops.

The only fresh water on a 19-kilometer stretch is a spring called Fonterra de Roland. It is on a hillside near deep woods, and it has seen countless pilgrims and soldiers throughout the past millennium. The spring is surrounded by an ancient stone catchment basin. The water flows slowly out of a pipe and into the basin. Everyone needs water at this point, so it is a likely place to meet other travelers and begin conversations. I met one couple from Germany who were filling up their water bottles at the spring. Although I never learned their names, I kept pace with them, our paths crossing several times, even staying at the same albergues on occasion, until we left the airport in Santiago.

The young woman was attractive, and I could not help occasionally watching her. Germans and other Europeans are not as modest as Americans. They will disrobe or change clothes with little to no inhibition. She was a pretty young woman with a firm and strong physique. She could have been a gymnast or model. Her blond boyfriend, about six feet tall, was also fit. During one of our short conversations, he told me he played a lot of soccer.

I also met Matthew, a veteran of the German army, at Fonterra de Roland. His soiled clothes were full of holes and tears. His hair was tangled, his backpack was dirty, and his walking staff was worn. Part of his left ear was missing. Small mementos, held on with string and leather ties, dangled from his walking stick. He started talking with me as we left the spring. Simon was still filling his water bottles and chatting with other travelers.

This was not Matthew's first Camino. He had started walking several years earlier. I complimented him on his English. He guessed that I was American.

As we walked together, Matthew's story unfolded. He was a soldier in the German army. He said soon after he returned from his second tour of duty in Afghanistan, he went into a deep depression. One incident in particular really messed him up. One day he was out on patrol with one of his buddies during his second tour. Up ahead was a dead cat lying next to a cardboard box. They stopped the vehicle and walked toward the cat because one of his buddies wanted to move it off the roadway. His friend was only a few paces ahead when he was blown up by the explosive device hidden in the cardboard box. The blast took his friend's head completely off. For 10 minutes, his body lay there, convulsing. After the blast, Matthew realized a small piece of shrapnel had taken off part of his ear. Another piece had passed through his leg.

When he returned home from war, he had a hard time acclimating to civilian life. He was living in Munich in southeast Germany, the capital of Bavaria. He started to do heroin. He knew he was severely sick. One morning he opened the door to his government-supplied apartment and started walking. He had been walking ever since, sleeping outside most of the time. He said he first walked to Santiago about three years earlier, then walked back to Munich. When he returned to his old neighborhood, he realized it had not changed. The drugs tempted him again, so he left within a month, walking to the Straits of Gibraltar and then to Lisbon.

On the pilgrim path from Lisbon to Santiago, Matthew told me he met up with another veteran, and they traveled together for about a month. One night a malnourished kitten came around. Matthew fed the kitten some of his provisions. In the morning, the cat was still nestled next to him but his friend had vanished without a word or any indication of where he was going. Matthew picked up the cat, and they traveled together for the next two years until he and the cat walked back to Germany. Matthew felt the cat was the spirit of his buddy who died in Afghanistan.

On several occasions, the cat warned him through body language when danger was ahead or if someone he met was not a safe person. He and the cat formed a strong bond. Matthew felt like he might be able to go back to civilian life again, perhaps get a job or go back to school. He wanted to contribute to society in some meaningful way.

Back in Germany, Matthew and the cat went out for a short walk one night, which they had done several times before. When Matthew returned from his walk this time, the cat was not by his side. He looked around for a few minutes, thinking the cat might have spied a mouse or gone off to explore. He went back to sleep, trusting the cat would be there in the morning. But the cat had vanished. Matthew went to pieces. He had lost his focal point, his only stability—he had lost his friend, again. He flashed back to Afghanistan, hallucinating that the cat was the dead cat, the one his buddy moved off the road just before his head was blown off. He realized the cat in Afghanistan and the one he found on the Camino were the same yellow color. The images kept haunting him.

Matthew decided to keep walking the Camino. He had little money and was sleeping outdoors most of the time anyway. He said he felt at peace while on the Camino, that his was a journey to live in peace.

We walked together for about 45 minutes while I listened to the story. Then, without saying a word, Matthews' pace quickened. He walked ahead and vanished. I never saw him again.

Nearly a week later, another pilgrim and I were having dinner. The other pilgrim had also met and walked with Matthew. We talked about him and his story. Even today, when I think about him, I feel a profound sadness for this wounded warrior. He had both emotional and physical scars. I should have offered him something more than an ear, given him some money or food. But he just left. I thought about the phrase from the movie "The Way": "One does not choose life; one lives a life."

TWO

RONCESVALLES

After Matthew vanished, I walked alone for a while. Simon had passed me and was somewhere ahead. We agreed our stop for the night would be the village of Roncesvalles, about eight kilometers ahead. It was late afternoon when I arrived. I met up with Simon at the entrance to the village. He was sitting on a stone block just past a small creek. One legend of the area I read described the defeat of Charlemagne and the death of Roland, his military leader, in 788 during the battle of Roncevaux Pass. Basque guerillas took Charlemagne's rearguard by surprise in a bloody battle. A small church is said to contain fascinating relics associated with the history of the village. At one time Roland's right hand and Charlemagne's chessboard were displayed in the church, but they are now lost to antiquity. Some legends tell of religious objects being hidden in caves in the surrounding tree-covered valleys.

As I entered Roncesvalles, a sign near a small gurgling creek warned of witches. It was a little unsettling yet fascinating to think that witches were thought to have roamed these woods 500 years ago. I wondered what a person did back then to be labeled a witch.

The largest albergue in the village is an ancient monastery that was constructed back in the 11th century. The walls are hand-carved stone blocks built to a height of 30 feet. The stone is a dense volcanic diorite, an intrusive igneous rock that will withstand weather for many years; the mortar will erode long before the rock. The walls are four to six feet thick. It's a massive structure and has protected monks and pilgrims for over 600 years.

The monastery recently went through an extensive interior renovation, which gives it a modern feeling. There are five floors with approximately 200 beds per floor. Each dormitory-style sleeping room has four beds (two sets of bunkbeds) with a small lockable cabinet for each occupant. You pay extra for the key. Each bunk has a charging station for a European standard 220v so travelers can charge their electronics.

It was a warm afternoon when I arrived. As I registered, I was excited about getting my *Credencial del Peregrino* stamped. The Credencial del Peregrino is a multi-fold piece of card stock, a regional passport to document your journey along the Camino. The *hospitalero* or attendant will check your official passport. They record your name, country of origin, and the passport number, and then stamp your Credencial.

THE PATH TAKEN

The stamp is unique for each albergue you stay in during your pilgrimage. The Credencial is a special keepsake documenting your journey and remains a special memory for years after.

After stowing my gear, I headed downstairs to look around. Standing in the foyer was a lady from Japan who I mistook for a volunteer. I asked her if she knew anything about muscle cramps. Luckily for me, her English was good. She worked for Visa credit card management in Japan. One of her friends joined the conversation and offered some special ointment from China that was good for muscle pain. They both seemed eager to practice their English, asking me where I was from and other general questions. After a brief conversation, they excused themselves to go to the dining room for the first dinner seating. We agreed to meet afterward.

Simon and I met in the lobby and decided to eat together. We were in the second seating. As you entered the room, you were directed to go left or right. Six people were seated randomly at each table. The tables had cloth linens and were set formally with a salad fork, dinner fork, soupspoon, table knife, butter knife, and a coffee/dessert spoon. The napkins were precisely folded. A dinner plate, salad plate, bread plate, and both water and wine glasses completed the place setting. All the chairs and tables were lined up perfectly. They could not have organized this area any better to fit more people comfortably. They probably had had lots of practice serving meals over the last 600 years. The floors were shiny stone, most likely polished by shoes of hundreds of thousands of pilgrims that have come this way.

The dinner was unexpectedly delicious. It was our first experience with the pilgrim menu, and it set a rather high bar for the rest of the Camino, as I would learn. Many establishments provide a pilgrim's menu, a nutritious meal for the cost of about €10 (euros). It typically includes protein, starch, vegetables, bread, and wine (or water). Our options this evening included potato soup, fresh green salad with a vinaigrette dressing, choice of trout, pork cheeks, or beef stroganoff, rosemary-garlic roasted potatoes, green beans, sliced baguette, red wine, water, and a peach cobbler for dessert. I had the trout, and Simon ordered the pork cheeks. If this was a typical pilgrim's meal, I would never lose weight.

The room was filled with lively chatter. I was excited, and I think others were excited to be on the journey. Although I was tired with sore aching muscles and hot feet, I was in good spirits. The red wine flowed liberally among the diners.

There were few paintings on the walls in minimalist décor, but they appeared to be original oils. Most were biblical themes of the crucifixion, the Holy Mother and Child, St. James, or a historic battle fought during one of the Crusades. Most were High Renaissance pieces, painted during the short period of exceptional artistic production in Italy in the late 14th and early 15th centuries. I wondered if they were on loan from a gallery in Madrid or perhaps from a private collection. Then it struck me: I was *in* the gallery. I was in the home of exquisite masterpieces. The paintings must have been on the walls for decades, if not centuries. I would see other beautiful and historic artwork, including stone and wood sculptures, in the smallest and most humble of churches, monasteries, and shrines. Many paintings were not roped off or guarded. The churches and cathedrals themselves were also architecturally and historically inspiring.

Most pilgrims dressed casually for dinner, including sandals. The conversation during dinner was lively, and you could tell people were excited to be on pilgrimage. I heard numerous languages, including French, German, Spanish, Italian, Japanese, and English. We shared our dinner table with two couples, one from Los Angeles and the other from Italy. We could not understand the couple from Italy but managed to use hand gestures and broken phrases to pass the food. I think they spoke a little Spanish, but they may have been too shy to use it.

The table conversation was one-sided for the most part. The man from LA was in his early 50s, slightly overweight with graying hair. He was a medical doctor. His wife, an investment banker, appeared to be a bit younger than her husband. She giggled rather than laughed. She was rather tall with strong, slender legs, auburn hair, and black horn-rimmed glasses. She had an inordinately large diamond ring. Something about her suggested she had an adventurous spirit.

We talked rather haltingly at dinner about what to expect during the next day's travel. We talked about the people we had met. In general, people seemed excited to be there, despite the uncertainty of what the days would bring. I was not sure what to think or expect. Travel like this was new to both me and my son. Neither of us had been on a pilgrimage before. I had done some backpacking and camping, hiking several miles per day in the wilderness. Physically, I felt good, weighing in at 195 pounds the week before we left. I had been riding my bike to and from work three to five times a week for the last five years, a 19-mile round trip. Despite the muscles developed from bike riding, after a full day of walking, my legs were tight with muscle cramps. I massaged them, but the cramps came back every day. They eventually subsided by the end of the journey. Simon, at 15, was entering the prime of his youth. My wife and I stayed busy driving him to and from soccer games, scouting activities, and various camps. He recently achieved the rank of Eagle Scout. He could do the physical challenge while I wanted to slow down and savor the experience.

I caught up with the lady from Japan shortly after dinner. Her name was Ming. In broken English, she said she was a schoolteacher. We walked up to her dorm room, where she produced a small plastic squeeze bottle of a clear ointment. She said it was an herbal mixture developed long ago, and it would help relax tight and sore muscles. She told me her father was a doctor of ancient Chinese medicine. Without blinking an eye, she sat down and applied the ointment to my calves, chatting as she did so. The ointment felt tingly on my skin, almost like bees stinging but not as intense. I don't know if it was the herbal mixture that helped or the massage of the muscles, but my legs felt restored within a few minutes. I no longer had cramps in my legs, but my feet were still sore from the walk.

I ran into Ming several more times during that first week. At one stop, I shared some cherries I had purchased. We talked about our families, and in broken English, she said she had two children but that her husband was not a good man. I could tell she was getting a bit emotional. Then Ming became quiet for a few minutes. Finally, she stood up and smiled at me. I stood up, too, and we gently hugged each other. Then she vanished around the corner of a building. I never saw her again.

After that last encounter with Ming, I thought about how people come and go in and out of our lives. I thought about Ming and about her circumstances. I thought about how human emotions can be diabolical and vicious at times. Our emotions cause us to ponder right and wrong, love and hate, life and death. If someone ever tells you they don't think about death and the end of time as we know it and what happens next, they are not telling the truth. Anyone who thinks long and hard about where we actually come from will know that we are stardust from the earliest dynamics of our galaxy, and it is to stardust that we shall return.

After visiting with Ming, I needed to do some laundry. I had only a few items of clothing with me. There were ten mechanical washing machines if you wanted to pay €2 to wash and €2 to dry. I used the washbasins as I did not have enough for a full load. A wire basket containing several soaps hung on the side of stone-carved water basins. I grabbed a bar with a strong scent of lilac. I have always found it odd that lilac belongs to the olive tree family and is deeply rooted in Greek mythology. The myth is that Pan made his magic flute from the hollow stem of the lilac plant. I thought of our lilac bush back home, and my mind wandered back to Corvallis and the rest of my family.

I wished they were with me. I missed Carole and Mateo, my younger son.

Washing laundry gave me time to reflect on many things. We were finally on the Camino. We had traversed a portion of the Pyrenees Mountains. I read somewhere that the first day is one of the toughest. It is. It is the first test of the pilgrim's physical condition. It was on the first day that I met Matthew. (And I would continue looking for him, hoping to give him some money.) Physically, I seemed to be doing well so far.

There are two answers to the question, "Where did you start your Camino?" One answer is you start from your home the minute you put your foot outside the door and leave your house. Using that measure, we were two days into our Camino.

I hung my clean clothes to dry and roamed around the ancient building. In one of the hallways was a large wooden box with a sign in several languages that read, "Leave what you do not need, take what you will need." How prophetic, I thought. The large three-foot container was overflowing with items people had decided they did not need after their first day. I went through the box more out of curiosity than need. The items included a sleeping bag, sleeping pads, razors, deodorant, towels, pants, underwear, socks, a toothbrush, hats, and a skateboard. The toothbrush gave me pause. Why would someone discard a toothbrush? Perhaps they had brought more than one. As I pondered the items in the box, I thought about what I needed versus what I wanted. My pack was heavy with gear, extra food, and extra clothing. I had brought several items that could be considered excess.

It was about this time I realized how tired I was. It may have been jet lag or the fact that I had not slept in three days, or both. I headed to my sleeping area, washed my face, brushed my teeth, rolled out my sleeping bag, and slept.

THREE

RUIZ AND PETER

On the third day in the village of Larrasoaña, I had a bit of a scare. I had warned Simon several times about keeping his passport in a safe place because, if he were to lose it, it would be difficult to get him back into the United States. He assured me he understood and would safeguard it along with his money. When one checks into an albergue, the host requests both your pilgrim credentials and your passport. They will write down your passport number and stamp and date your Credencial de Peregrino. If anything happens to you (like if you disappear), the authorities track your path by way of your last passport entry. It's pretty smart, when you think about it. It provides a layer of protection and security.

As I was checking into the albergue in Larrasoaña, I could not find my passport. I took everything out of my Osprey backpack with its 10 external zippers and a zipper pocket inside of a zipper pocket. I spent 30 minutes digging through my pack to no avail. I asked the hospitalera to call back to the last place I stayed. She explained what had happened over her phone, and they agreed to look in the bunk area I had stayed in the previous night in Roncesvalles. Meanwhile, I was checked in and shown to my bed. I kept thinking of what I would tell Simon.

The Credential del Peregrino is a 3-by-5-inch paper document purchased for two or three euros. It is folded in an accordion fashion to display nine pages with six squares outlined per page. Starting from the small ancient village of St. Jean Pied-de-Port in southwestern France to Santiago de Compostela, each place you stop for the night has a personal stamp. It is an actual inkpad handstamp, nothing electronic. Each mark is individual and intricate in detail. Some stamps depict a church structure or castle in the town. Others are quite simple with a cross or some other distinguishing feature. The stamp tradition dates back to the Middle Ages when the Knights Templar needed a way to distinguish a pilgrim from a peasant looking for a free meal or shelter. This document allows for physical interaction with the hospitalero, your host for the night. The hospitalero tells you the rules of the facility and shows you to your bed. Your interaction with the hospitalero helps them manage the facility and keeps pilgrims from randomly selecting beds. Some hospitaleros are volunteers, providing a genuinely marvelous service to pilgrims. They keep the albergue clean, orchestrate communal meals, provide directions to the pharmacy, church, or grocery store, and offer a prayer and opportunity for self-reflection. Self-reflection is one way the Camino helps the pilgrim slow down life.

Inside the Credencial del Peregrino is the Pilgrims Prayer. The prayer dates back to the Codex Calixtinus, written in the twelfth century to provide background detail and advice for pilgrims. I prayed it whenever I attended a pilgrim's mass. It is a beautiful prayer, recited by a priest at the end of the service. It reads:

> God, You called your servant Abraham from Ur in Chaldea, watching over him in all his wanderings, and guided the Hebrew people as they crossed the desert. Guard these your children who, for the love of your Name, make a pilgrimage to Compostela. Be their companion on the way, their guide at the crossroads, their strength in weariness, their defense in dangers, their shelter on the path, their shade in the heat, their light in darkness, their comfort in discouragement, and the firmness of their intentions: that through your guidance, they may arrive safely at the end of their journey and, enriched with grace and virtue, may return to their homes filled with salutary and lasting joy.

Once in my sleeping quarters, I went through my pack again. Inside a zipped ultra-hidden pocket was my passport. I went and showed the hospitalera. She called Roncesvalles to report it found. She must have been thinking, "Dumb American." I chuckled about this incident but never told Simon.

After I showered, I rinsed out my few articles of clothes. The sun was bright, the breeze warm, and my clothes quickly dried. I asked the hospitalera about a place to eat, and she directed me to a market at the far end of town. It was about 5:30. The main street was completely vacant. It was uncomfortably warm. It felt good to be wearing clean clothes, but the pavement was hot, my feet were sore, and blisters were breaking out in earnest. I realize now I should have taken better care of my feet.

Some women were walking out of the market as I approached. We greeted each other with smiles and nods. It looked like they had been shopping for dinner supplies; one of the women clutched a bottle of wine and another had a baguette.

The market was attached to a small courtyard protected by eight-foot walls. Along the perimeter of the yard were several old fig trees, and a variety of flowers growing in red clay pots dotted the area. It was pleasant. Entry to the courtyard was through weather-worn wooden gates. The market was near the far left back corner. Several red plastic tables were scattered around, each with a MAHOU BEER red-and-white hand-cranked umbrella rising from the center hole. The open umbrellas looked like red and yellow Indian paintbrush plants growing in a desert garden.

I picked up some Calabrese salami, Havarti cheese, tomatoes, a banana, and a baguette. I also bought a one-liter plastic bottle of water. I knew I wasn't drinking enough and needed to stay hydrated. This plastic bottle was to be with me until I returned home. I refilled it countless times.

The storekeeper watched me impatiently, seemingly annoyed. It felt like I was more of a nuisance. Then I noticed the soccer game, and I realized he was preoccupied with the game between Real Madrid Club de Fútbol, the national soccer team of Spain, playing the team from Nigeria. I quickly learned that the FIFA World Cup was in full swing and would continue through the first month of our journey. Simon and I would be caught up in the frenzy of the competition.

I made my way to a shaded table outside where I could keep an eye on the game. It was late in the afternoon, and I was the only one in the place. No sooner had I sat down and started to make myself a sandwich when a woman with sandy blonde hair entered through the gate. She smiled at me and headed into the market. I heard her speaking loudly in Spanish to the shopkeeper. When she came out, she smiled at me again, then came over and introduced herself as Ruiz. She had purchased some dinner supplies much like mine, but she also had a bottle of red wine. She asked if I had a corkscrew. I did. I opened the bottle for her, and she offered me a glass. I offered her some water. As we chatted, two young women went into the market. We recognized each other from the albergue. They had been washing clothes while I was frantically searching for my passport. They exited the market with wine, bread, cheese, and lettuce. We invited them to join us.

When I was preparing for the trip, I read that if you have a corkscrew, you are an instant friend to everyone. So before I left St. Jean Pied-de-Port, I purchased a Swiss Army knife with a corkscrew. It was true! As I opened bottles, the conversations flowed. Most travelers had started the pilgrimage in St. Jean Pied-de-Port. Ruiz was from this area of Spain, Basque country. The other two women were from Italy and spoke good English. They were primary school teachers. In fact, several of the travelers were schoolteachers of one sort or another. It seemed they all had the summer off or at least a good portion of it. As we talked, three more pilgrims from Canada came into the courtyard. After they shopped they, too, joined our table. Then another young pilgrim from Australia joined us. The shopkeeper came over with a plate of olives, a sliced baguette, and a plate of olive oil. He was delighted to have the business. Several more people arrived and found nearby tables.

Pretty soon the air was filled with a cacophony of English, Spanish, or German conversation, all with a common thread: the pilgrimage. Everyone had questions. The table was a beehive of excitement with everyone sharing food, wine, and conversation. It was like a United Nations dinner party, filled with engaging and spirited accent-ridden banter. I found myself sitting back and just listening.

My thoughts drifted to Simon, and I wondered how he was doing on his own. I managed to get an email to him. He responded that he was with the Shade Brigade. He said he was okay and not to worry. I hoped he was having a good time and engaging with people as I was doing. Despite his reassurances, I worried about him.

After about 45 minutes at the UN party, I excused myself. I needed to finish my laundry and prepare for the next day. To be truthful, I was tired. It was the end of a long, hot day. I had walked 24 kilometers, lost and found my passport, but most serious, I had lost my son. St. James, the patron saint of the Camino, was setting the tone for our journey. I packed up my leftovers for lunch the next day. As I was leaving, I said goodbye to Ruiz as she rolled another cigarette. Everyone wished me *Buen Camino*. This phrase means "good road" or "good path" and is the traditional farewell to pilgrims along the way. I walked back to the albergue alone with my thoughts as the sun was setting.

I didn't sleep well. The dormitory room with 16 beds was a little noisy with people snoring or coughing, but really, I was more concerned about my son. Finally I drifted off, glad to be off my feet for the night. I woke up early to the crow of an overzealous rooster. People were already milling about in the dormitory, and the snoring was fading away. I pulled on my hiking shorts, stepped gingerly into my shoes, then headed to the bathroom to pee. My feet were incredibly sore. The blisters were swollen with clear fluid, and I started to have doubts that I would be able to walk the remaining kilometers.

After packing my gear, I departed the albergue and headed out of town before the sun had come up. Within about three kilometers, I entered the ancient-looking village of Akerreta, where I stopped at a small bar for a café con leche and something to eat. Café con leche is a delightful coffee brew that I like with just a touch of sugar. I also ate a slice of a Patta Grañón, made of boiled potatoes, chorizo, onion, garlic, cheese, milk, and butter, and baked into a casserole. The café used local ingredients. I must have been really hungry because I could have eaten twice as much.

I met Ruiz again as day was breaking. We walked and talked together for a long while. Her English was excellent. She rolled her own cigarettes, smoking one after the other like a walking volcano, and her fingers were stained a dull, dingy yellow. She was a high school physics and English teacher. She enjoyed hiking in the mountains and whitewater rafting. She was from a small village, about 75 kilometers away. Her family had always been from the Basque region of Spain. She lived in the same village where her mother, grandmother, great-grandmother, and great-great-grandmother lived. She had never considered leaving, other than going to Madrid University and walking the Camino. Every year she walked for two weeks and then returned home, planning to walk the next section the following year. That is what her mother had done years before. She was walking alone right now, but she planned to meet her boyfriend in a few days. They would hike together and return home in about a week. She had also met Matthew, the wounded veteran from Germany. We briefly talked about him. We shared numerous other random encounters along the trail.

About 10:00 a.m., we stopped to rest outside a café. Ruiz continued talking while having café con leche. Several other pilgrims joined us at our table as they rambled into town. Before long, our small gathering grew to 11, including people from France, England, Australia, Canada, and Germany. It was hard to say how long some of the other travelers had been on pilgrimage. Most of us drank coffee, but Peter, who wore a gaberdine uniform and smoked a cigar, ordered schnapps. Ruiz continued smoking her unfiltered cigarettes like they were candy. Ruiz and Peter spoke as if they might have known each other previously, based on the intensity of their conversations.

Peter was a big man, about six feet four inches and around 50 years old. He spoke English with a heavy accent. He told me that he started walking from his home in Zurich. He decided to walk the Camino following his recent divorce. He had quit his job at a financial firm about three months earlier. I saw him several times in the first few days and soon realized he had slept in the same albergue that Simon and I slept in the first night in St. Jean. We always acknowledged each other and had stilted conversations. He told me he was not particularly religious, so I asked him on several different occasions why he was making this trip. All I ever got in response was an unenthusiastic "for the exercise" because he needed to lose weight. Yet he managed to be eating or drinking whenever I encountered him, and I started to doubt his stated reason. Our paths crossed every day until we reached Burgos.

THE PATH TAKEN

When we arrived in Burgos, Peter stated that he was going to stay over. He admitted that he had taken a bus part of the way. He sounded sad that he had caved into the temptation to ride a bus, something I was seriously considering due to my blisters. He said it was a consistent pattern of his life, that he always quit things that were important to him: his most recent marriage, his previous marriage, this pilgrimage, his job, and any other significant challenge. He seemed to get more depressed as we talked.

I listened, sipping my coffee as he spoke. When I finished my drink, I picked up my gear and prepared to leave. Peter had already started a conversation with a Canadian woman at the next table. They were laughing, and I heard him order a beer. I interrupted his conversation to shake his hand and wish him Buen Camino before I walked away. I never saw him again.

After thinking about some of the things Peter told me, I wondered if he had done some bad things to people. Perhaps he was involved in corporate fraud or embezzlement. Maybe he had raided a company's pension funds and left people without any retirement income. That would be mean, though in hindsight, I'm not sure anything he told me was true.

FOUR

CIZUR MENOR

No matter how hard you try to manipulate the future and plan it out, you just can't do it. Something will change and it will not work out as planned. I cannot tell you how many hours I put into looking for the perfect walking/hiking shoe for the trip. By the fourth day on the trail, I had blisters so bad that I felt like quitting and riding the bus to the next town. The temptation to take a bus or taxi crept into my thinking on several occasions, mainly because my feet were in such pain. I even went so far as to look for a bus stop. But I didn't. I walked every step of my Camino on foot. I knew other trekkers were worse off than I was.

My feet looked like I had leprosy. My toes were so swollen they looked like mature well-fed Chihuahuas. My feet were so swollen they would not fit into my special expensive, well-researched Salomon Cross-trek shoes. I decided to wear my sandals for a few days. I probably spent €200 on first aid supplies for my feet over the course of the trip. I bought gauze, tape, Betadine antiseptic, Band-Aid bandages, Compeed blister cushions, ibuprofen, and eventually, new shoes.

When I stopped in Cizur Menor on the evening of the third day, Simon was with me, and he could tell my feet hurt. I asked if he had any blisters, and he said no. His old running shoes were working well for him. An older lady named Claire was the owner of the albergue, which had been in her family for over 200 years. Albergues are often private businesses, but they might also be owned by a municipality, a convent or monastery, or a Spanish federation. We chatted for a few minutes in Spanish. She could tell I was in pain and offered to look at my feet. Later that afternoon, she drained the fluid out of my blisters with a small syringe and then handed me sanitary napkins to put into my shoes to cushion the bottoms of my feet. She told me to buy more sanitary napkins to absorb the fluid that would continue to drain over the next few days.

So I did. I felt a little funny walking around on sanitary napkins. I wondered if she told all the pilgrims the same thing as a kind of mean joke. She would call her friends and tell them that today she had 30 pilgrims supporting the sale of sanitary napkins in the Basque area of Spain. To be totally honest, she did this service for free, though she did have a donation box. I appreciated the attention.

Out in the various courtyards, pilgrims had hung out their clothes to dry. Several of the walls were in ruins, and it was clear that some had been large dormitory-type rooms in years past. A pond in one of the garden areas looked like it had been a swimming pool at one time, but now water lilies were growing in the pond, and a number of rather large turtles, 10 to 12 inches long, lived in the cool murky water. Claire pointed them out by name: Paco and Menno, then Tule, Juanita, Berta, and Beanie, or something like that. It was hard to understand her as she spoke English with a very heavy Spanish accent.

As we were talking, she said it was time to feed the turtles, and she invited a young pilgrim girl to help her. I think the young girl was from Romania. As I watched the routine, the turtles came to a certain section of the pond at feeding time to chomp down on canned dog food, for which they had developed an insatiable fondness. They were fed from a metal spoon. Over time, Claire had trained the turtles to come to the sound of her spoon tapping on the side of the can. The turtles battled aggressively for the moist morsels of protein. Claire told the girl to put the dog food on the spoon at the edge of the pool, but instead, she put it on her finger. Claire warned the little girl not to do that because "a turtle bit my finger off." The girl, a little horrified at the sight of Claire's missing digit, picked up the spoon again.

Simon and I washed several articles of clothing

and hung them to dry. The wash basins looked old and well used. Then we headed across the street to a restaurant for dinner. My feet were throbbing, even though I had changed into sandals.

I could not sleep that night, despite the warm, gentle breeze blowing through our dormitory room. I had not yet discovered the pain-inhibiting power of 600mg of ibuprofen. Instead I tossed and turned from the pain of blisters, sore muscles, and aching joints. As I lay awake in bed, I grew more and more restless. Finally, at one o'clock in the morning, I quietly woke Simon and whispered for him to meet me outside without his gear. I told him I could not sleep and needed to leave. He could take care of himself in the morning. I would be down the trail a bit and would keep looking over my shoulder for him. I told him my feet were in bad shape and I would slowly try to make it to the village of Puenta La Reina, about 20 kilometers away. I handed him €200 and told him to spend it wisely. We hugged, he went back to bed, and I packed my gear and headed out.

Walking at night is a mysterious exercise. I walk at night back home, usually during hunting season. It is amazing what you hear: birds singing, frogs chanting, flies buzzing, dogs barking, cats fighting, crickets chirping, the wind blowing, and people singing.

Coming out of Cizur Menor going west, the

road has a gentle and long gradual upgrade. One of the guidebooks I read described a lone monastery on this section of the trail. I saw the lights from a great distance. They looked almost alien in color, a strange iridescent blue glow. The small monastery is set deep in the hillside to the north. The monks there offer shelter to pilgrims and have done so for centuries. I thought I heard faint Gregorian chanting as I walked the trail, a mystical, almost scary wisp of melodic winds.

There was a cross and monument on a knoll near the asphalt road that led to Galar. It caught my eye because of the moonlight. I thought it might have been the road to the monastery. The monument marked this area as the place that Charlemagne's Christian army defeated the Muslim army of Aigolando in the 8th century. In the wee hours of the morning, I could almost hear the cries of dying soldiers from the wars hundreds of years ago. They seemed to echo on the gentle breeze. Their bones had turned to dust that now lay scattered in the soil of unmarked graves along the roadside and in the fields. In the daylight it would have been impossible to hear the whispers of the night. But darkness sharpens your senses, allowing you to feel more than you see. Your imagination creates fear in your mind when vision is limited.

It may seem like a random thought, but maybe

the sense of chaos that surrounds the Camino is what contributes to its mystery. The days begin to blend together. I wondered about the power of St. James that draws people from all over the world to do this pilgrimage. The reasons must be both spiritual and mystical. But what drives people to make certain decisions? The reasons for choosing one action over another are a complex puzzle. Many people make the pilgrimage. But how many have done this walk in the past? Over the last thousand years, millions have made this journey. I felt like I was part of something much bigger than myself.

When talking with fellow pilgrims, I sensed that many people think about quitting the walk after only a few days or a week. I knew deep in my heart I was not going to quit. But I was tempted. Something inside me wanted to quit. I started asking myself why I had taken the time out of my life to do this. I had put everything on hold to make this trip happen. The logistics that went into planning something like this were overwhelming, but something inside kept me going. One traveler I talked with said it was the pull of St. James that manifests as an overwhelming desire to fulfill a commitment to one's self.

After I heard this, I thought back to another period in my life when I drifted spiritually. I was living in Austin and had recently exited the military after a three-year commitment. I was probably drinking a little too much in those days. I was lost in the sense that I had no true direction. One day I ended up at a Catholic church that overlooked Lake Travis. I talked to a priest and I told him I wasn't sure why I was there. I made my confession, stating that it must have been 10 years since the last one. He told me I was there because it was the pull of God bringing me back to the church. He said God would always pull me back because he was my creator, and humans have a spiritual nature that yearns for connection to our past and a power greater than ourselves. I have thought about that conversation many times throughout my life, and recalling that phrase, "the pull of God," during the Camino really resonated with me.

The pull of something greater is a concept I have always struggled with. Probably many people do. What can explain the pull other than God? But something deep in my spirit was stirred up at that time, even though I could not understand it. I did the penance the priest gave me to absolve my sins. In the Catholic religion, you do penance for your sins in order for your sins to be forgiven. My penance was to go to a children's hospital and visit a sick child, to go see a child who has no hope of living a full life.

I put off the penance until 2017 when I went

to the Doernbecher Children's Hospital in Portland. I met with a chaplain. I told her why I was there. She told me about a Hispanic family with a four-year-old daughter who was dying of leukemia. She was in bed when I met her, being held by her mother. Her father and brothers were also in the dark room. I prayed the Our Father with them in my broken Spanish. Although I did this as a form of penance, it did not feel like it was enough. Did I learn to be thankful for the blessings I have?

I was in the midst of the magic of the Pyrenees foothills. This area is the beginning of the Mesa de los Tres Reyes, the tabletop of Spain. The topography changes to rolling hills. Your perspective changes with it, and you begin to question your motives. The walk can become tedious with all the ups and downs. As you adjust to the monotonous grind, your mind and emotions seethe and twist around and around with the intensity of an F5 tornado. I did not notice the distance as I walked each kilometer. Most of the time I was deep in thoughtful contemplation, in solitude, in peace with sore feet. Yet the rhythm of footsteps and randomness of thoughts sent me into a place that was frothy and confusing. I heard the birds singing and I watched them darting in and out of sight like the sparks from the embers of a fire. I noticed how many crosses there were scattered randomly along the way. Most marked a place of death. Pilgrims had stacked stones on the arms of the cross or at the base. Some of the crosses had thousands of rocks piled on and around them, each rock a prayer or special intention for someone who was loved deeply or perhaps even hated. The Bible says to love your enemies.

One cross stands out in my mind along a particular section of the Camino near the village of Atapuerca. This area is significant because of the archeological history that has literally come to the surface. The region has been inhabited for well over 850,000 years, and the hand tools found in caves are said to be spectacular. While researching for the Camino, I was fascinated by the discovery of stone tools in this region.

Viewing an Internet photo image is not the same as standing in the presence of such magnificent ancient works of art. I felt as though I could understand the thoughts of the creators of the tools and the processes involved in the creation of this work. I could almost imagine what they were thinking and what drove them to develop tools 850,000 years ago. Archeologists have found skeletons in caves around the area, human evidence of the existence of this community. I was walking on the same hunting ground as those ancients from hundreds of generations past. The thought that this place may have contributed to my own existence captivated me. The animals that were hunted and killed nourished my ancestors from long ago. My DNA was linked to these ancient people. I was experiencing a strong déjà vu. I had been here before.

I gazed over the landscape, imagining the herds of deer or antelope grazing on the knee-high grasses swaying in the afternoon breeze of distant lush green hilltops. Pockets of scrub-type oak trees would have dotted the hills, much like they do today. Perhaps the weather was cooler and the people wore animal skin for protection from the elements. The hunters would have had well-chiseled faces and tough dark skin due to the continual exposure to the weather. Their blades would have been made from dark chert or flint, their long shafted spears at the ready. Neanderthals wandered Europe 850,000 years ago, wearing animal hide moccasins lined with fur. These people were my ancestors, and here in this place I felt a strong connection to the life that teemed here thousands of years ago. In my mind I saw the families gathering around the fire in the evening, eating the day's kill, telling stories of the hunt, launching into the legends and stories of their forebears, developing a fiction for the next generation to grasp onto and pass on to the next.

The cross, as I recall, was on a hillside. It was old, and rocks of all sizes and shapes had been piled up around its base. The geology of the hill was karst, an irregular limestone with white jagged edges Swiss cheesed with holes from erosion. This rocky formation would shape and delineate the trail for many kilometers.

I sat at the base of the cross to rest for a short time. It was a cold morning with the wind blowing, but the sky was crystal clear.

It was at this resting place that I met Saratoga. He was sitting at the base of the cross when I arrived, and it looked like he had been there a while. Speaking in Spanish, he told me he was 85 years old and from Barcelona. He said he had been an art student all his life, and this was the fourth time he had walked the Camino from St. Jean Pied-de-Port to Muxía and back. He told me a story about his first Camino at the age of 22. As he gazed into the distance, he recalled a man he had met and the story he told. Ancient hunters in this area used a special tactic to rustle up big buck deer to kill. Saratoga pointed to an area past an old broken-down barbwire fence. The view was obstructed by tree, but I could see what appeared to be a cliff about 150 yards away. Saratoga motioned for me to come with him. I grabbed my backpack, water bottle, and trekking pole and followed him. We climbed over the barbed wire and stood at the edge of a cliff that dropped about 80 feet. We hiked a well-worn pathway along the rocky karst cliff to a box canyon. As we walked, he explained

THE PATH TAKEN

that hunters of ancient times, when humans were first using fire, had learned about cooking meat. This area was one of the first places that fire was utilized. The canyon had once teemed with carnivorous wild animals, including cave bears, saber-toothed cats, hyenas, mountain lions, and wolves. Although we had larger brains and walked upright, it was an extremely competitive world, and humans were fair game. The only real law was the law of survival.

Saratoga had learned how to call up wild animals. Ancient hunters could mimic the sound of a rutting buck using a series of sounds. Saratoga asked if I wanted to hear him do it. I nodded yes. He had me sit down, then put his finger to his lips and waited for quiet. Just when I thought he had been pulling my leg, Saratoga let out a series of grunts, then let go with "O-o-o-o-ah-ah-ah-ah-ho-o-o-o." A shiver went down my spine. A few minutes later, he let out another call, "O-wah-o-ah-o-ah-w-o-o-o-wah," paused briefly, then again called out, "O-wah-o-ah-o-ah-w-o-o-o-wah." A few minutes passed. I started to think nothing would happen, so I motioned to Saratoga with my thumb that it was time to get back to the trail. He stayed me with his stare, and I froze. On my right, I heard branches breaking in the distance. The sound was getting closer. Saratoga called out again, "O-wah-o-ah-o-ah-w-o-o-o-wah, O-wah-o-ah-o-ah-w-o-o-o-wah," and then louder, "O-o-o-o-ah-ah-ah-

ah-ho-o-o-o." That's when I glimpsed the 12-point antlers of a huge buck. He snorted and pawed at the ground, ready to fight. The buck looked around for his challenger. Then the wind shifted a bit and he picked up our scent. With a snort, he vanished silently into the dense vegetation.

Saratoga motioned for me to follow him, and we climbed out of the canyon. I felt at peace, like I had been here before. We climbed up the hillside toward the cross where we had met. Saratoga told me he had shared this story and side trip with only two other people over the years, and I was the third and last one he would ever tell. He said the old man who taught him had only shown three people, including Saratoga during his first Camino at 22. Like Saratoga, the old man had walked the Camino four times. Why I had been brought into this secret fraternity, I had no idea. Was it my ancestors pulling me back?

I woke up with a jolt, the dream crystal clear in my mind. I had fallen asleep at the base of the cross. I needed to write down the dream while it was still fresh.

When I stood up, I saw other travelers moving down the pathway. Simon was standing next to me. He said I had been sleeping for about 15 minutes.

FIVE

ALTO DEL PERDÓN
(Mountain of Pardon)

On the third day of the journey, I left Cizur Menor in the darkness. It was 1:00 a.m. I started the gradual climb to the top of a mountain pass named Alto de Perdón. As I walked in the dark, I heard the ghostly whooshes of far-off wind turbines. Every now and then, a measured burst of red light flashed a beacon of warning to low-flying aircraft. The massive blades swooshed rhythmically, a foreign sound in this ancient area. Perhaps pilgrims of times past would find the wind turbine a good idea.

The mountain pass is at an altitude of 2,560 feet. It is home to a collection of three-quarter-inch thick iron-sculpted silhouette figures of pilgrims, their heads bent westward as if facing a gale force wind blowing east. The figures at the front are outlined in ancient historical clothing, and they progress in succession until the last figure appears in modern attire. As you gaze westward into the distance past the sculptures, lights of villages can be seen many kilometers away.

Alto del Perdón is a special place. It marks the transition of the Pyrenees into rolling foothills before reaching the Meseta, the large and expansive flat plains of central Spain. It is the second phase of the Camino de Santiago. Numerous monuments, obelisks, markers, and signs are fused into the contours of this area, and the wind blows constantly with great intensity. It is a great location for wind turbines.

The trail on the back side of Alto del Perdón continues at a steep grade. Loose rocks make it a challenge for sure-footed walkers, but it is an even more difficult walk for those with blisters and raw feet. I pulled out my headlamp to aid my descent.

As the day gathered light and early morning twilight transformed the dark, I found myself on a narrow trail sewn into a steeply sloped valley wall dotted with rock stacks. People had taken time from their journey to stack three, four, five, six, and even 20 rocks on top of each other. I have been on mountain hiking trails with similar cairns and markers. As the daylight grew, I realized there were thousands of them. They were everywhere, accumulated over hundreds of years. Some were made of big boulders, and others were merely pebbles. A large number of them had token objects or photographs attached. Each stack had been placed with special intentions. And now these thousands upon thousands of intentions were hemmed into the fabric of this holy place.

I quickly realized this was a sacred place, and I felt a strange and mysterious connection. No guidebook had mentioned this place of remembrance. I thought of Ishmael's words in *Moby Dick*: "It is not down in any map; true places never are." Clearly, this was a true place. As I walked down the mountain into the valley, I felt the urge to create a stone cairn of my own.

When daylight finally peeked over the cloudless horizon, I stopped to rest and pray for a while. A cold razor-sharp wind rushed past my ears. I sensed the whispered voices of people all around me as they prayed with intentions of hope, peace, strength, and forgiveness. I built a small cairn five stones high and prayed for my family: my wife, my sons, my mother, my sisters, and my brother. I prayed for my cousins, aunts, uncles, and distant family that I did not know. I felt certain that my ancestors had walked this path before. I sensed they had stopped and built rock markers as well. I wondered if it was this one or that one or another one. They, too, would have prayed for their families long ago and prayed for future generations to come. They must have prayed for forgiveness of past transgressions and failures that impacted their families, as did I. Then it struck me that I was the next generation, the one that followed them. Likewise, I prayed for generations yet to come. I wondered if St. James was using his discipleship as a message: to the pilgrim to follow in his footsteps, and to their families to believe in the power of God and faith.

I didn't realize how tired I was until I finished building the cairn. My feet were throbbing and pulsing with pain. The cold wind was still screaming by my ear. I found shelter by some large rocks and shrubbery about 30 feet off the trail. The clearing was relatively flat, and I brushed away the loose debris. Situating my backpack as a pillow, I put on my jacket and curled up to sleep.

I dreamt of vivid reddish pillowing clouds rushing past in a sky of deep azure. In the distance, lightning burned the sky like blue iridescent alcohol. Hundreds of faces of people I did not know flashed like strobe lights across my eyes. Some faces were old and some were young. Men, women, and children flashed across my mind's eye in brilliant colors, exact details, and tangible textures. The dream was more like a hallucination, and I recall it vividly, as though it was a message of some kind. As I write this story, I still search for the meaning and intent of the dream. It was one of the most powerful visions I have ever had.

I must have slept for about an hour or so. When I woke, the wind had died down completely. It was ghostly silent. Nothing moved, not even the wind turbines. I sat up, surveying the area. The sun shone brilliantly, but the air was still crisp and cool. I ate a Cliff bar and drank some water, all the while marveling at the hundreds of thousands of rock cairns that surrounded me. After thinking and meditating awhile longer, I put my gear away, slipped on my backpack, and standing, bid the spirits of my past to rest in peace.

The view to the west was unobstructed. To the east was the long tedious slope of Alto del Perdón, its massive wind turbine fins circling rhythmically in the sky. The tri-blade wind machines reminded me of Don Quixote and Sancho Panza jousting with windmills in the old story. The face of the mountain was imposing in full daylight, and I was glad I had traversed it in the dark.

The experience of that early morning still haunts me. I felt a connection to something far greater than I. The intense joy of joining my past and seeing the future is something I will never forget.

My day would end in Puente La Reina, is about 20 kilometers from Cizur Menor. I still had a long way to go. My feet were swollen and raw. The fluid from the blisters on both of my feet was still draining onto sanitary napkins. They were terribly uncomfortable. The skin on my right foot was folding under, and every step brought a sharp shock of pain. I decided to stop and change socks.

While my feet aired, I pulled out my pocketknife, sterilized the blade, and carefully cut away the shriveling skin. I applied some Betadine to the open wound and taped gauze to both of my feet. My feet were so swollen, raw, and painful that I could barely fit them back into my shoes. It didn't seem possible that I would make it all the way to Santiago de Compostela, and I considered stopping or taking a bus.

I lifted my backpack and slowly began making my way. Each step was a deliberate effort, but with each one I made progress. I did not see anyone else until around midday when I stopped at a small village for food and water. I purchased a *bocadillo* and sat by a fountain near the center of town.

A bocadillo is a sandwich of ham or salami or turkey with cheese served on a sliced baguette or roll. It's similar to an American hoagie but not as loaded. In some markets you can have it made to order, but many times the bocadillo is prepared ahead of time and you get what is available.

While I was eating, a pilgrim approached me and told me about two doctors in Puente La Reina who could examine my feet. The doctors were hospitaleros in a large government-funded albergue on the west side of the city. The doctors worked for free or for a small donation, if a pilgrim is so inclined. The pilgrim's name was Bryan, and he was from Ireland. We shook hands. I

THE PATH TAKEN

thanked him, and he walked off down the trail in the direction opposite from where I was going. He must have been on his way home.

After lunch I resumed my walk down the pathway. The sun had warmed the air. It was late June, and the heat of summer was palpable throughout the land. Flowers were blooming, and farmers rode slow, mule-paced tractors to plow their fields. The terrain was changing. I started to see vineyards. As I continued west, the landscape was filled with vast oceans of wheat undulating in the soft summer breeze. The slopes of the hillsides were gentle and inviting to the weary pilgrim. I thought of the bread and wine that came from this region and how the Catholic mass transformed such simple gifts into the body and blood of Jesus Christ. This connection would linger in my thoughts for the next 563 kilometers, giving me a powerful sense of religious connection to the Camino.

As I climbed the gently rolling wheat- and vineyard-covered hills, Puente La Reina appeared down in the valley, the Arga River (Rio Arga) coursing through the center of town. I reached the albergue Bryan had directed me to, and sure enough, two Belgian doctors were the assigned hospitaleros at the facility. They were laughing and conversing with trail-weary trekkers as they arrived and checked in. One of them played a well-aged guitar plucking out a welcoming *ostinato*. I learned that these doctors had been coming here for two weeks each year for the last 20 years. They provided a valuable service for no stated charge, and they helped pilgrims with just about any medical, logistical, or relationship problem. By now, many other pilgrims had developed severe blisters, shin splits, or other common ailments associated with long-distance walking on uneven surfaces.

I spied Simon playing soccer on a grassy area with some fellow travelers. Somehow he had passed me on the trail, and it was just coincidence that we ended up in the same albergue for the night. We talked for a few minutes. He had been invited to cook dinner with his friends, and they would watch the World Cup soccer match later in the evening. I could tell he was having a good time. His face was tanned, and he seemed to be enjoying his independence with his new band of colleagues. I told him my feet were in a bad way. He told me his feet were fine, and blithely turned to rejoin the soccer match with his friends.

After I registered and paid the €8 fee, I received my bunk assignment. I asked one of the doctors if he could examine my feet. We arranged to meet in a couple of hours as he was busy checking in pilgrims. While I waited, I took a shower and washed a few articles of clothing.

Soon enough, one of the doctors, Dr. Deslaugh, called me into an examining room. He looked to be about 60 years old. As I removed my sandals and washed my feet, he told me about his home, why he was here, and what had motivated him. He worked as an obstetrician, and his partner was a neurologist. He and his friend decided to serve other pilgrims after they completed their first Camino about 22 years ago, and now they came back every year because they had grown to love the service they provide. They meet interesting people from all over the world. They had seen an incredible increase in the number of pilgrims since their first Camino.

As we chatted, the doctor cleaned my feet, looking for signs of infection. He noted an area of concern on my right big toe and told me to keep an eye on it. If the infection became worse, I could end up in a hospital without completing my pilgrimage. He wrapped my feet and told me to keep the bandages on for the next two days. I was to purchase additional gauze and tape at the pharmacy in the next town and change the dressings, keeping my feet as clean and dry as possible. He said my feet were bad, but that he had seen a lot worse over the years. One man he treated a few years ago had developed gangrene and had to have his foot amputated in Madrid.

I thanked him and asked how much I should donate. He smiled and told me whatever my wallet could afford.

SIX

AGNES

As I left the doctor's examination room at the albergue in Puente La Reina, I saw a woman with vivid green eyes checking in, getting her Credencial stamped and her bunk assignment. She wore light gray hiking shorts and a multi-colored scarf wrapped loosely around her head that fell gently over a simple white V-neck t-shirt. Despite her simple attire, she was elegant. Her red backpack looked worn but not shabby. When she smiled at me, a lock of blondish hair fell out of her scarf. Her cheeks were red and flushed from the heat of the day. I would later learn that her beauty was from deep within.

I did not speak with her until the next morning. I limped out of the albergue on another cool and cloudless day. We happened to be leaving at about the same time. In her native German, she said she understood why I was walking so gingerly. She was also concerned about blisters, but she was well prepared and so far had not developed any issues with her feet. She walked patiently beside me as I struggled to keep up with her without letting on that every step was agony. We managed to converse, though my German was rusty and she spoke only a few phrases in English.

I found Agnes engaging. Over the course of the Camino we randomly met, walking sometimes in conversation and sometimes in silence. Certain things about her struck me as curious and delightful. She wore very little makeup, yet exuded simple elegance, an air of refinement, sophistication, and grace. As I mentioned previously, Europeans are much less inhibited than Americans; they disrobe or change clothes with little or no thought of being watched. On one occasion when we stayed in the same dorm room, she emerged from her bed and began doing yoga in her underclothes, which she presumably had she slept in. I watched her briefly before averting my gaze. She was beautiful.

I felt a budding attraction and speculated on "what ifs." What if Agnes found me interesting? What if our friendship was on a track to something more? I felt an unexpected stir of emotions, and I quickly snapped back to reality. It was absurd to consider anything more than a platonic relationship with this young lady. Back in Oregon was a wonderful woman whom I had made a promise to, and although our 20-plus-year relationship had been through many bumps and trials of will, I was not going to jeopardize it. Over the years Carole and I had been married, we have had some wonderful times. We have camped, hiked, biked, cooked, cleaned, traveled, and built a safe, humble, and comfortable life. We were blessed with two strong, healthy, smart boys, one of whom was with me now. Carole and I are a team. We work together, save together, and plan our future together. Don't get me wrong; our relationship has seen both good days and bad, but we have kept our promises to each other. As the sun sets at the end of the day and we climb into bed together, we clasp each other to share warmth. We are at peace most of the time, we are friends most of the time, and we are lovers. I can rest with Carole at the end of the day, knowing my conscience is free from guilt. Our relationship is like a strong tree. With each passing year, we add another ring of growth to our relationship, making it stronger. The winds will blow and the rains will fall, but so will the sun shine, and we will smile through it all and grow old together.

My commitment to Carole was strengthened by the fact that my parents had gone through a long, drawn-out messy divorce. I look back on how it affected me and my siblings. It was an extremely bitter time in our lives, and I knew early in life that I never wanted to get divorced because I did not want my children to go through what my siblings and I had. When parents divorce, it is the kids who suffer the most. They are the real victims. They wonder their entire lives if they could have done something to keep their parents together or if they were the cause of the split. I am vehemently against divorce: nobody wins, and it's a scar on the lives of all those it touches.

I went through a divorce after my first serious relationship. My first son Max will suffer the results of the breakup the rest of his life, and there is nothing I can do about it. I regret I do not have a stronger relationship with him. His mother Bonnie and I had irreconcilable differences. That is another chapter.

I had no intention to pursue Agnes or any other woman, despite the temptation. I was on a spiritual pilgrimage. Agnes was no more than a beautiful temptation. Her voice and delicate smile, her slightly pursed red lips and green eyes captivated me. I grew quite fond of her, but our age difference was over 30 years, and besides, I was happily married. The only thing I could offer was to listen quietly and patiently, enjoying the company of a beautiful woman. If she asked, I might offer her advice based on the many mistakes I have made. That was the best I could offer.

Pilgrims who meet on the Camino will discuss any variety of topics, and so it was with me and Agnes. One clear and cool morning, after breakfasting on a café con leche and croissant, I was on the trail, deep in thought, and battling philosophical questions of life. I heard footsteps behind me, and then I heard Agnes' guttural yet dulcet voice: "Guten Morgan."

As we walked, we talked about our lives. Agnes told me she worked with troubled youth ages 7 to 18. She enjoyed the work, especially the ability to develop trust and make a connection with young people who had had a difficult life. Many were from broken families and had been abused sexually or emotionally or both. Her job was to develop trust, becoming a friend, mentor, counselor, and confidante. She was completing her studies at the Leibniz University in Hanover, working as an intern outside of school. Her field of study was psychology, specifically the adolescent years.

One time I asked Agnes why she was walking the Camino. She explained it was just because she wanted to. She was drawn to do it; it was an unexplainable pull. She hoped to find more meaning in her spiritual life, to find truth in the simplicity of life. Although she was religious, she had not practiced her faith in many years, explaining she was more of an Easter and Christmas kind of Catholic. Yet she also felt that the Camino was changing her faith somehow.

She told me she was seeking out some of the places her father wrote about in his journals and asked how I felt about World War II. I said I was interested but not a scholar on the subject. My father had served in the Asiatic-Pacific Theater, and his brother Muaro was lost at sea when his B-29 bomber was shot down. After that, we walked in silence for a long while.

As we entered the small village of Lorca, we both needed to find a restroom. That meant we would likely have purchase something from the shopkeeper, which I assumed was customary. I learned it was not expected, that many shopkeepers along the Camino understood the need of pilgrims, and they would rather you use their facility than go outside and dirty up the place. Although I enjoyed my conversations with Agnes, I decided I would rest a bit and told her I would meet her down the trail in a while.

SEVEN

SIMON

When I first began planning my Camino, I asked each of my family members if they would like to walk with me. I was surprised when no one jumped at the chance. It was Europe after all. I had lived and traveled in Europe as a child. My father was stationed in Germany while he was on active duty with the US Army. We vacationed in a Volkswagen camper bus we fondly named "The Catacomb" because the six of us slept in layers of bedding throughout the vehicle. My little sister slept on the floor, my parents in the main cabin across a table area, my other sister across the front cabin area, and my brother and I on the top bunks. We traveled across Europe, stopping at castles, vineyards, cathedrals, crumbling medieval ruins, museums, battlefields, and remnants of buildings blown up during World War II. We visited Rome, Paris, Luxembourg, Barcelona, Madrid, Amsterdam, Lisbon, Pisa, Gibraltar, Berlin, and many other cities and villages. We went to museums and historic structures, such as the Louvre, Heidelberg Palace, and Dracula's castle with medieval torture devices in the dungeon. We rode the slide into the salt mines in Berchtesgaden and had a somber history lesson at Hitler's Eagle's Nest retreat. We visited cathedrals, including St. Peter's Basilica, Notre Dame, and countless others. We played around bombed-out bunkers along the Siegfried Line and found spent bullet casings and other war artifacts in a farmer's field. We camped in the dark and ominous Black Forest. We learned to ski in the nearby Bavarian village of Altglashütten and camped in Italy with the Boy Scouts. We swam in the Mediterranean Sea while at summer camp. My childhood friends and I roamed the German countryside playing army. It was a childhood that I learned later in life to savor. Because of my experience, traveling in Europe was comfortable for me.

The trip I proposed was going to be an out-of-the-box adventure with a purpose, so much more than a vacation. Most kids today think a vacation is lying on a tropical beach and reading a book or two. I think a vacation should be a learning experience, an opportunity to explore and indulge in the culture and customs of another country. My first son from a previous marriage, Max, lives in Canada. We've never had much of a relationship. I thought this adventure might give us an opportunity to know each other better. He said no, he had to work.

HECTOR RODRIGUEZ

In my immediate family, no one was interested in going except Simon. He approached me after my initial invitation, and after asking a few questions with some hesitation, told me he would like to go. I was excited. It would be a father-son trip. Afterwards when I thought about it, I wondered if Simon was going for the adventure or perhaps going so he could look after me. Simon was 14 when we started planning. He had a lot going on with school, soccer, Scouts, and activities with his friends. He had recently completed a seven-day, 65-mile backpacking trip in the Eagle Cap Wilderness in northeastern Oregon with five of his scout buddies. He was in great shape, and I had no doubt he could handle the Camino.

As we planned, Simon asked questions about food, gear, and other logistics. What would we eat? Where would we sleep? What was the weather going to be like? He had all the basic gear, including a 56-liter backpack and good boots, although he hiked the entire trail in Nike running shoes. I needed to get him a passport and get mine renewed. I could do just about everything online. The Internet is a unique and wonderful resource.

Simon had grown into a highly spirited young man with a quick humor and genuine heart for others. He is smart, confident, and forthright. He has an easy smile and an intuitive sense of others in distress. He is fun to be around. As we planned our trip, I grew more excited to have him as a travel partner. At least that was my vision. After we started walking the Camino, we did not spend much time together. After the second day out, we got separated when I missed a turn. Although we maintained communication through email, we did not walk together at the outset. I thought about him a lot as I walked alone. I had read that the Camino has a certain magic about it and that miracles happen to travelers on the Camino. Things happen when they are supposed to. Sometimes they cannot be explained but rather must be lived and experienced.

With Simon's youthful legs and long stride, it quickly became apparent that he would walk at a much faster pace. I was going to have trouble keeping up with him. On the first day, I watched him move up the side of a mountain with graceful ease as I lagged behind panting, sweating, and stopping to rest. As the distance between us increased, I thought of it as a metaphorical inference on the outcome of our walk. He moved ahead seeking new adventures around the next turn on the path of life and while I, on the other hand, had a slow and measured paced. I was older and my joints were achy. I took the time I needed, and he moved on with the frenzied pace of youth. I wondered if the distance that separated us was an indication of how our paths might diverge in life. I understood from my interactions with my father that, as our children grow up, they are supposed to leave us. As parents we prepare our offspring as best we can to wrestle with life's challenges. We do what we can to protect them, arm them with lessons from our mistakes, and pray that their path will be better and more fulfilling than ours. He and his brothers are the legacy of my bloodline, and I hope that line continues long after I am gone.

Alone with my thoughts, I soon found myself reflecting on experiences with my father. My father was a Simon and so was his father, my grandfather. My dad passed away in 2005 at the age of 76 years. He was an attorney and had practiced law for over 50 years. He spent most of his career providing legal advice to the military. I reflected on the legacy he had left me and my siblings.

I am a prisoner to the things my father valued. Sometimes I feel as though I am hostage to his hopes for a legacy. So many awkward conversations were left hanging because I did not understand him. I crumpled up letters that I meant to send him, giving him my point of view about life's challenges. I thought he did not understand me. In hindsight, I realize it was my own inability to understand the wisdom he tried so hard to share with me. As an attorney, words were his life. He had a deep understanding of history.

He kept files, including dossiers on me, my brother, and my two sisters, as well as a number of other people and things. He seemed to know what was important to save and what was okay to toss out. On one of my last visits with him, he wanted me to take custody of the family files. I did not fully understand why, but it was important enough to him that I did it.

I realized, after my dad passed away, that he was wise. He lived a good life and provided for our family of six as best he could. His anger never lasted. I only wish I had realized sooner that we were simply not going to see eye to eye on everything, and that was okay. I wish I could have told him that when he was alive. I am sure Simon will feel the same way at some point.

As I watched my son stride confidently ahead, I knew things he did not: that he would experience love with its happiness and pain; he would ask questions of life; and if the good Lord permitted, he would have a loving family of his own one day. I wanted my children to feel fulfillment, just as my father did for me and his father before him. Yet I could not help but feel a bit melancholy. What legacy would I leave him, his brother, and future family generations?

I hope and pray that Simon has a life of adventure and curiosity. I hope I continue to always be part of his life. I truly believe he will be a good man, a true and trusted friend, a man of good character, and that he will live a life of adventure and compassion.

On our first day out, Simon met several young adults who became his Camino buddies throughout the journey. Although he was the youngest of the group, he managed to fit in. This is the group I previously described as the Shade Brigade. We had wonderful sunny weather throughout the entire trip. It rained for maybe 30 minutes during the entire 40 days. We had prepared for much worse, bringing rain pants and jackets. The Shade Brigade continually looked for shade from the hot Spanish sun. They were a close-knit unit that took care of each other.

One of the members was Jens, a 28-year-old German man. He was about six feet three inches with blond hair, blue eyes, and a well-built physique. He spoke good English, and we had numerous engaging conversations. I suspected he had a strained relationship with his father. I could tell that he respected his father and wanted his approval. Jens had served in the military and was currently attending university in Munich to study engineering. He played a lot of soccer. He wasn't sure what he wanted to do with his future but hoped the pilgrimage would provide some answers. He didn't speak of his religious beliefs, but it was obvious he thought deeply about his relationship with God. He and Simon became good friends, despite the difference in age.

Huy from Houston was another member of the Shade Brigade. He appeared to be in his mid to late 20s. He was of Asian descent with a fun yet confident air about him. He was always quick to help others, and I could tell by his gear that he had researched and planned extensively for the trip. He was a technology wizard. He had the latest electronics, including a solar charger, backup batteries, smartphone, an extra phone in case his smartphone died, and a backup GPS tracker system. He knew how many steps it was to the next village, town, or city. He could tell you to the minute how much daylight we still had. He could also tell you what was going on in the presidential campaign back in the US, including what brash, demoralizing, degrading, and confounding rhetoric Trump was spewing. He was also a very good cook. During my conversations with him, I learned that he had a deeply religious upbringing. He attended mass and received communion frequently during his Camino. In the evenings, we had serious philosophical discussions. When he returned to the US, he planned to work in Washington, DC.

Another member of the Shade Brigade was Maggie. She was a tall and slender 19-year-old woman from Ottawa, Canada. She wore her hair in dreadlocks. Her legs were long, strong, and tan. She planned to attend university in the fall. She seemed to be from a well-to-do family as she talked about other adventures and travels. She had been to South America, Africa, the Far East, and various places in the United States. She was well-rounded and could converse on a variety of subjects. She was a free-spirited person who carried herself with an air of confidence. If she had any fears about traveling alone or being intimidated by others, it didn't show.

Clinton disappeared and reappeared intermittently. He was another free spirit from Chula Vista, California. While others hurried down the trail, Clinton stopped to smell the flowers, identify a singing bird, study tree bark, and photograph anything else that drew his attention and curiosity. He ventured off the trail and into the fields to sit or sleep. Once he broke out in song in his loud baritone voice just for the joy of singing. What most people noticed about Clinton was his long, thick brown hair.

My German friend Agnes slipped in and out of the Shade Brigade easily, like a ninja. She, too, became friends with the group.

The 15th day out, Simon and I ended up together again. I was glad to have his company. I suspected he was low on money, so over dinner I gave him another €200, just in case we were separated again. I wanted to spend some time with him, and he agreed. I knew he could take care of himself and told him if he wanted to walk with his friends, that was cool, too. However, the Shade Brigade decided to layover in Leon for a day to tour the city and visit the beautiful cathedral.

We officially entered the Meseta at this point. *Meseta* translated from Spanish means "tabletop." This topographically flat region of northern Spain seems endless. When we were there in June, some areas were covered with golden wheat fields as far as the eye could see; there were no fences to speak of. The sun was often brutal, and potable water was scarce on some sections of the trail.

When Simon and I were finally able to spend time together, we often walked in silence. It was strange. We occasionally had conversations about our family back home and wondered what they were doing. We talked about my past and what his future might hold. But much of the time we walked in silence, and that was okay.

I typically rose before the sun and started out on the path alone. I stopped for a quick coffee and pastry with other early risers I had come to recognize, and continued down the trail. Simon slept a bit later, until about 9:30. He rose, did his wakeup routine, and headed out. He inevitably caught up. We walked together for a while and discussed a plan for the day. We stopped for food, looked at the maps, referenced our guidebooks, calculated the distance we could comfortably cover. Then he resumed his pace, moving swiftly down the way. I watched him stride confidently out of sight. If he stopped for café con leche or water or soda or snack, sometimes I could catch up. I was surprised at how much ground a person can cover when just walking. My average distance was 15 to 20 kilometers a day, though I subconsciously stopped counting each passing kilometer. Fifteen to 20 kilometers seemed like a reasonable distance for someone in good health.

Simon and I tried to meet up around noon for lunch. On several occasions we simply found a market and purchased lunch supplies; a baguette, some hard salami, cheese, nuts, and fruit. We looked for a fountain in a churchyard or a spot of shade near ancient Roman ruins and ate together. We might catnap after lunch in the warmth of the day. Every now and then we found a bar with a lunch menu. Simon discovered a traditional dish called an *Ensalada Mixta* that included fresh lettuce, carrots, beets, tomatoes, cucumbers, onion, Spanish olives, tuna, and was drizzled with olive oil and balsamic vinegar. This salad became one of his favorite dishes. To this day, he will occasionally create an Ensalada Mixta for his lunch at home.

Although we traveled at different paces, we achieved many significant milestones together.

THE PATH TAKEN

The path at the entrance to the province of Galicia is marked with prominent kilometer posts indicating the distance to Santiago de Compostela. We hit the 100-kilometer post together, and we entered Santiago de Compostela together. We visited the cathedral and the tomb of St. James together. I watched Simon as he knelt in the crypt a few feet away from the Apostle James's remains. He was very respectful and reflective of this time and place. He spent a long time in silence, staring and praying at the foot of the ornate silver casket that held the remains of a man who knew Jesus of Nazareth.

We took a photo when we reached the 0.0-kilometer post together at Cape Finisterre. We looked out over the Atlantic Ocean, the ends of the earth, together. I think the simple times we spent together will be the lasting embrace of this journey. The milestones we reached will always resonate with me. I hope and pray he will one day bring his own son or daughter on this pilgrimage and share the valuable time with them. I will always treasure the memories we created, and I hope they will always bring a gentle easy feeling to Simon as well, that he will understand the importance of sharing adventures and time with people you love. We may not always see eye to eye on things, and that's okay because we have shared this experience together.

EIGHT

FATHER IGNACIO AND THE SUNGLASSES

After a long day and steady but gentle upward grade, I arrived in the medieval village of Belorado. It was day 11, 4:00 in the afternoon. It was here I met Father Ignacio, priest of the parish and hospitalero of the albergue I checked into. His voice was a rich baritone. He was the only priest in the area and responsible for three churches. He had recently finished daily mass. I am not sure why we connected, but we talked for about an hour. I followed him around while he did some chores. I offered to help; he declined but said the company would be appreciated. After the last mass of the day, he admitted he was a little tipsy, due to all the wine he consumed while performing the rites of communion for his flock. Most of his congregation were older ladies. I told him about my family back in the United States, and that my son Simon was on his own Camino somewhere ahead of me. He listened intently and said he wanted to visit the US someday. His own family was from Málaga in southern Spain. His father was a carpenter. Two of his brothers were also priests, one serving in Brazil and the other in Africa. Three other brothers lived and worked in Burgos.

We talked for some time about the perceived weakness of faith in the younger generations. Although most of his flock consisted of older women, he hoped the younger generation would one day return to the church.

The conversation soon shifted, and he began asking questions about new developments in technology and other things I might know about. He pulled out his iPhone to check his messages. The screen was cracked, but it didn't seem to bother him or interfere with the operation of the phone. He told me he was an avid reader of *Wired* magazine and was surprised that I subscribed to it also. He seemed a bit nerdy and asked lots of questions. I thought he might have made a good spy or counter-intelligence officer.

Father Ignacio told me about Belorado and the albergue where I was staying. The dormitory was part of a church built into the side of a limestone cliff. Belorado's albergues, churches, and hospitals have provided a resting place for pilgrims for over a thousand years. The church at the foot of the cliff was originally a hospital. The facing plaza was lined with a variety of shops, bars and restaurants. It resembled a medieval village. The town is in a steep valley carved out by the Tirón River (Rio Tirón). We entered the sanctuary of the Church of Santa Maria, genuflected, and crossed ourselves. Father Ignacio busied himself at the altarpiece etched with images of *Santiago Matamoros y Peregrino*. He began resetting the alter for mass the next day.

The Church of Santa Maria was built in the 16th century. It was modest but felt warm and inviting. Several beautiful works of art, including original oils and numerous marble sculptures, adorned the interior. One sculpture was of the Virgin Mary with child. Father Ignacio told me about caves at the top of a cliff behind the church. The caves were once home to hermits and were heavily used as shelters during the Middle Ages. Even today a pilgrim might find their way to the caves for shelter. He offered to take me to see the caves, and I agreed.

We were joined by another pilgrim from Italy, who also spoke Spanish. His name was Nadal. We climbed an ancient staircase that took us around the right side of the sanctuary and through a private garden area. At the far side of the garden, a heavy locked gate was bolted to the side of the cliff. Father Ignacio took a ring of about 20 keys from is pocket, located a skeleton-type key, and unlocked the gate. It creaked loudly as he swung it open.

THE PATH TAKEN

We climbed 200 well-worn stone steps that were carved into the cliff wall. The air was cool and damp. Rounding a corner at the top, I spotted several good-sized natural caves. The largest appeared to be about 30 feet deep and 20 feet across. According to Father Ignacio, thousands of pilgrims had sheltered here overnight, including, apparently, the hermit San Capraiso. Like others before him, San Capraiso was martyred for his faith and subsequently became the patron saint of the pilgrim route to Rome, the Via Francigena.

The cave felt like a holy place. The walls were chiseled with dates, names, and other marks, like ancient graffiti. The ceilings were about 25 feet high and blackened with soot from fires used for cooking and warmth. Two fire rings had been built from carefully placed limestone rocks. The concave walls provided numerous sleeping areas. I thought about the stories the walls might tell if they could speak and about the people who slept there. Their spirits were present in the nooks, cracks, and scratches in the walls.

The entrance looked out to the west, into the sunset and toward Santiago. We looked out to see the Camino trailing to the west, encompassing the horizon. Father Ignacio pointed out a monastery on a distance hillside. On quiet nights, he said, the gentle breezes carried the sound of the monks singing Gregorian chants to the village below.

We continued climbing to the top of the cliff above the caves. The Father showed us castle ruins and walls next to the Tirón River on the western side that were built to defend the village. Nearby was the convent of Our Lady of Bethlehem (Nuestra Señora de Belen), as well as a Roman army encampment established in 1230.

As the sun reached the horizon, Father Ignacio spoke in a hushed and somber voice. Pope Innocent III had used this site as an outpost, an office away from Rome. Pope Innocent III was one of the most powerful, bloody, and influential popes ever, going to extremes to spread Christianity throughout Europe. He claimed supremacy over all of Europe's kings and queens. He was responsible for the deaths of thousands of Jews, Moors and pagans. He organized the Fourth Crusade as part of an overall strategy to attack Jerusalem through Egypt and take holy relics back to Rome. It was a bloody time in Catholic history.

Due to failed military strategies and poor intelligence, a small troop of renegade Crusaders found their way to Constantinople and sacked the city in 1204. These Crusaders brought their plunder home. According to legend, much of it was hidden in the hills around the area, but no one has ever found it. Some believe one of the cups from the last supper is hidden somewhere in the hills.

As I looked out to the west, I asked about the

lights off in the distance. Father Ignacio pointed out the Convento de Santa Clara about two kilometers away. A modest monastery was also visible on a far hill. We lingered another 20 minutes, watching the setting sun cast hues of soft red and blue across the western sky. Then Father Ignacio hurried us along; he had another mass to perform.

We made our descent and soon reached the albergue. I just had time to thank Father Ignacio for the personal tour before he jumped on a blue Vespa motor scooter. The tail pipe was attached to the frame with bailing wire. As he rode off, I heard him yell, "Buen Camino!" Nadal and I made our way back into the dormitory where several other travelers had arrived and were settling in for the evening. Some were cooking dinner in the communal kitchen. Most everyone looked a little road worn. I needed to tend to my blisters; although healing, they still needed attention. I headed to the showers. It was also time to wash some clothes again.

Doing laundry had become a regular event. Socks, shirts, shorts, and undergarments always needed washing. All albergues have some sort of clothes-washing facilities. Some have machines; others have simple stone-carved washbasins. On day 11, I had settled into a routine on the Camino. I was about one-third of the way to Santiago de Compostela.

I returned to my bunk hoping I could find out where Simon was. I wrote him a short email about what town I was in. Within a few minutes, I received a response. He was in Belorado as well, only a few blocks away. The Shade Brigade had found an albergue with a swimming pool, charging stations right next to the beds, and a large grassy area where travelers could get massages for a nominal cost. I headed over to check on him.

Most of the pilgrims at this albergue were young, mostly in their 20s. Simon seemed to fit right in. He had learned to juggle at a young age and was putting on a show for people around the pool. I watched him while I enjoyed a cold beer. I could have gone for a swim but I was enjoying the delicate dance of life that was unfolding before my eyes. The young pilgrims were eating, reading, doing laundry, juggling, swimming, and laughing. Several were on their phones. These young people socializing in a global community gave hope me for the future. The world needed more opportunities for this type of engagement. We would all benefit from making new friends across the globe.

I was road worn, dusty, and tired from the day's hike. I was also a little mentally drained. I had much to reflect on from the day's walk. I thought of my family and how I came to be here. I thought about why I was here, but I had no clear answers. I pulled out my journal and wrote some notes by the pool. After about 30 minutes, I told Simon that I was going to find something for dinner and go to bed early. He was going to cook dinner with his friends and invited me to stay. I passed as I needed to wash my clothes and hang them to dry in the warm Spanish evening air in order to prepare for the next day. I said I would look for him in the morning and advised him to make wise choices. We hugged and I walked back to my albergue.

I felt good about leaving Simon to explore his new freedom, have new experiences, and build new friendships. I trusted him to make good decisions. It was time for him to grow in self-confidence as a young adult. Maybe it was time for me to let him go without constantly watching over him. It was a time of growth for both of us.

I slept well and woke around 6:00 a.m. and was out the door by 6:30. I felt rested and prepared for the day with new energy. I checked my guidebook and map; I was still 630 kilometers from Santiago.

Within a few minutes of starting off, Agnes joined me. We talked a little about the albergues and dinners we had enjoyed, but otherwise we walked together without talking much for a long time. The silence was good. We established a good pace, the ground crunching rhythmically with each step.

Simon and several of his friends caught up about

HECTOR RODRIGUEZ

9:00 a.m. We had stopped for coffee and food in the town of Todos Santos. As soon as he joined us, he realized he had left his sunglasses back at the albergue. When I purchased the shades for him in St. Jean Pied-de-Port at the beginning of our trek, he promised me he would not lose them. He immediately said he needed to go back and find them. It was about eight kilometers back to Belorado. I told him, not to worry, that they would probably be gone, picked up by another pilgrim. Instead, he and his friend Jens started to run back. They found the sunglasses on the table beside his bed. Then they ran back. It was a 16-kilometer round-trip run, but they were back within an hour and a half. I will always respect that about Simon; he will do his best to keep a promise.

NINE

TODD AND SILVIA AND BRUNO

It's the people you meet that make the most lasting impressions. They come from all walks of life and from across the globe. I met Todd the morning I left León. I guessed he was about 30 years old. He taught Spanish at a high school in the heart of New Jersey. He had a slight build and a full red beard, like a young Ernest Hemmingway. He had an infectious laugh and a face that contorted into all sorts of sinister expressions of inquisitiveness. Although currently unmarried, he was in a serious relationship.

Back when he was in high school, he decided to take Spanish to fulfill an elective. His teacher was passionate about teaching, and Todd fell in love with the beautiful imagery and poetry of the language. He earned his bachelor's degree with a major in Spanish, then went on to earn a master's degree in Spanish culture. He was on summer break, as were many of the people on the Camino.

Todd had spent several summers in Spain. He had heard of the Camino de Santiago some years earlier, but this was his first pilgrimage. He first planned a trip with a girlfriend three years earlier, but the relationship ended on a bad note and his original plans fizzled out. The relationship ended because of his obsession with bullfighting. During a summer trip to southern Spain, Todd was invited to a bullfight. The performance sparked an interest in the pomp and ceremony surrounding the duel between the bullfighter and a 1,500-pound beast.

Todd described the mystique and history of Spanish-style bullfighting, which is also known as *las corridas de toros*. or "running of the bulls." Bullfighting dates back to pre-Roman times and is popular in Mexico, Colombia, Ecuador, Venezuela, and even France. At first the sport was reserved for the very rich. Charlemagne is said to have enjoyed it. El Cid, a knight and warlord in medieval Spain who fought against the Moors, was considered the greatest Spanish bullfighter. According to legend, El Cid had an uncanny sense of timing and killed over 200 bulls during his lifetime. He sounded to me like the Russell Crowe of the Middle Ages.

As I listened to Todd's stories, the kilometers passed quickly. He described the three phases of the fight with each phase signaled by bugle. In the first phase, *tercio de varas* (the "part of lances") the bull is released into the ring while the matador and the banderilleros observe how the bull reacts to the colorful capote or red cape. During this stage the bull is stabbed by mounted picadors in the *morrillo*, a mound of muscle on the neck of the bull. This is the moment that blood is first drawn. The bull becomes more animated and lowers its head in a show of aggression. Then the bugle sounds, signaling the second stage, the *tercio de banderillas* (the "part of a small flag"). The matador attempts to plant two banderillas (barbed sticks with red flags) between the shoulders of the bull, which weakens the bull through the loss of blood while also making it even more aggressive.

The third stage, the *tercio de muerte* (the "part of death"), is again signaled by a bugle blast. The matador re-enters the ring with a small red cape (muleta) in one hand and a sword (estoc) in the other. As the matador teases the weakened bull to charge, he stabs the bull again in the morrillo, piercing the aorta or severing the spinal cord to end its life quickly. The matador's reputation is based on his ability to give the bull a quick and clean death with the final thrust of the sword. If the bull is not killed quickly, the matador is booed and will not rise to be a master of the sport. On some occasions, the bull will gore and even kill the matador. Bullfighting is not a sport for the weak of mind or stomach. Timing and skill is everything. Killing a hundred 1,500-pound bulls is quite a feat for the career matador.

Todd's passion and keen understanding of Spanish culture was fascinating. I felt that he had perhaps been born at the wrong time and place in history. He was a fascinating blip on the screen of life.

Every pilgrims moves at a different a pace along the Camino, and when Todd and I reached a lull in our conversation, he said he was going to stretch his legs and walk ahead. Once he vanished over the horizon, I did see him again on the trail.

I entered Villar de Mazarife early that afternoon. Todd had arrived earlier and was in a bar talking with some locals. As I set my pack down, I heard "Ector!" It was Bruno and Silvia, an Italian couple from a small village in northern Italy. I met them early one crisp morning about five days into my Camino. The sun was just cresting the eastern skies, casting a pastel pallet of reds, pinks, and ocean blues. We watched a squirrel gather walnuts in a small grove.

Bruno was strong in body and spirit, in the prime of his life. His long hair was tied off in a black and white bandana. Silvia had dark curly hair, also tied back with a bandana. Her simple attire enhanced her shapely body. As they walked past me that morning, they were holding hands. It was a beautiful picture of a young couple in love.

Our paths crossed many times during my Camino, and we frequently stayed in the same albergues. Every time, they were holding hands.

They carried full backpacks, yet they synchronized their walking pace. Although their English was limited and peppered with Italian phrases, we learned a lot about each other during our encounters. Sylvia worked as a technician in the field of art preservation, restoring paintings. Bruno was a civil engineer and helped to maintain the village infrastructure.

As we neared Santiago de Compostela, Bruno announced that he and Sylvia were going to be married. He invited Simon and me to the wedding. I made a note of the date and time in my journal. On the day of the wedding, we met them outside the cathedral. Bruno asked me to be his best man and witness. Of course I said yes. And so on July 24, 2016, in the chapel of the Blessed Virgin Mary at the Santiago de Compostela Cathedral where the Apostle James is said to be buried, Bruno and Sylvia recited their vows in Italian during a short ceremony. It was a simple ceremony but beautiful. Sylvia looked so beautiful and happy. Bruno was proud of his bride. She was a good person. I hope they are living happily ever after in northern Italy.

As Simon and I entered the last third of the Camino, the terrain became more rugged and mountainous with both coniferous and deciduous trees. This region is where it is said that your spiritual canvas begins to take on colors. Hues of spiritual awareness take on more form and intensity. It was day 18. The journey's physical end was in sight. I thought about the many gifts of kindness I had received along the way. I recalled the many people who had walked a portion of their journey with me and thought about why their stories resonated. I pondered how I may have impacted other pilgrims. I thought about the albergues I had stayed in, the hospitaleros who ran them, and the stamps in my Credencial.

The tradition of providing hospitality to pilgrims on the Camino de Santiago goes back over 1,000 years. Hospitaleros are special caring people who choose this noble way of life. They often devote their entire lives to serving the pilgrim. That being said, being a hospitalero can be good business, especially by the last 100 kilometers when the Camino is crowded and the albergues are often filled to overflowing. During the early and mid-summer months especially, throngs of students scramble to complete the last measure of the journey in order to receive their Compostela certificate, proof of their struggles on the Camino and acknowledgment of a merciful God. One can earn a Compostela by walking at least 100 kilometers or biking 200 kilometers.

TEN

CRUZ DE FERRO

The Cruz de Ferro, located between Rabanal del Camino and Ponferrada, is a solitary iron cross that sits atop a 10-meter wooden post. It is the highest point on the Camino de Santiago. The post is gray and cracked with age. It must be 450 to 500 years old. Its ancient fissures house troves of sacred notes, photos, and charms left by believers.

There are numerous theories about the origin and symbolism of the cross. One theory asserts that the cross was erected to guide pilgrims, particularly in the winter months when the route can be obscured by snow. Another theory suggests that the cross was erected during Roman times to mark the border between territories. Still another claims that, because it is the highest point on the Camino, it is where pilgrims are closest to God, where He hears your prayers more clearly. A pilgrim who walks the Camino with a penitent heart and prays for his merciful forgiveness at the Cruz de Ferro will be forgiven for their transgressions.

I was awed at the sight of the Cruz de Ferro.

Stones of every size, shape, and color were scattered on the mound. Photographs, letters, and notes littered the area. People had left ribbons, rosaries, small religious medals, dead and wilting flowers in the massive mound of stones. I found myself praying for hope—hope that my life might be of value. I asked God to show our family how to listen for the answers we were seeking, to help us have the wisdom to understand. I believe that, at some time in the future, God will show us his mercy.

Many pilgrims carry a stone from their home to symbolize the burdens of life that will be left at the foot of the cross. I carried four such stones. My mother, who was 85 years old at the time, gave me three small limestone rocks, each about the size of a quarter, from her garden in Texas. When I planned my Camino, I told her about my research on the Cruz De Ferro. When she gave me the stones to carry, she never told me what they meant, and I could only imagine things I knew about my mother that lingered in my distant memory. I do know that she grieved deeply about three miscarriages she experienced early in her marriage to my father. I know she and my father went through a messy divorce when I was in high school. Although he never struck my mother, he lashed out with words, which can last much longer. The anger between them had been building for a long time. During and after the divorce, they fought court case after court case until my father died. Their battles impacted all of us kids in one way or another. It was not a very pleasant time for our family, so it's possible she had some remorse and sought forgiveness. I imagine any person wanting to be forgiven of past transgressions can recall all the sins of their lifetime. Since I did know the specific sin for which my mother wished to be forgiven, I prayed for her to have peace during the twilight of her life. I prayed that the burdens of her life would be lifted, that anyone she may have harmed would forgive her, and that she would forgive anyone who had harmed her.

I also carried a stone for my own sins, which are many. Could I have been more honest in my life? Could I have been more trustworthy, loyal, and helpful? The answer to each of these questions is yes. I have never killed anyone or knowingly hurt anyone physically (except for Ronald Bradford in elementary school; he was a bully). Could I have been a better husband or a better father? Could I have been a better son, brother, cousin, or uncle? Could I have been a kinder man? I know in my heart I could have. But how does one make amends to those whose paths you will never cross again? We live day by day and try to make the best of the gifts we have been given. Some days we are more successful than others.

As I placed my stone at the foot of the cross, I prayed the Lord would see it as a symbol of my struggles on the pilgrimage. I prayed that when we are judged at the end of time, this pilgrimage would tip the balance in my favor and I would enter heaven. I knelt in silence for what seemed to be a long time, knowing I needed to do better with my life. It was a moment of great personal reflection.

Simon watched as I placed the stones at the foot of the cross. He had carried his own stone. I never asked what it meant to him. He placed the stone solemnly, and then he prayed.

As you approach the Cruz de Ferro, you are shrouded with a feeling of calm. It is a sacred and reverent place. The number of stones is a testament to the millions of souls who have walked this way. Each stone represents the burdens, pains, sorrows, tears, and sins of the person who made the journey. Some stones are quite large. They must have been large burdens to carry.

After placing our stones, Simon and I retreated to a table under a shelter to rest a while. The sky was overcast with deep gray billowing clouds. The cold wind blew briskly. I was relieved that I had made it to the cross.

As we left the Cruz de Ferro, two young ladies moved down the trail at the same time. We had met Traycee and Karole a few days earlier in León when we stayed at the Parador de León. The Parador is one of the most beautiful Renaissance buildings in Spain and was once the headquarters of the Order of Saint James, whose soldiers provided protection to pilgrims. The original building was demolished in the 16th century due to its age and ancient design. Work on the present-day structure began in 1515. As you walk through the interior, you are greeted with stunning artwork. Each public room is filled with paintings, stone carvings, armor, tapestries, and heavy dark wooden furniture. The floors are polished marble, and the walls convey a sense of deep and rich history.

Although the rates were high, we got the pilgrim discount. It was still a splurge. We each had our own queen-size bed with soft sheets, cotton towels, and a television. When I arrived, Simon was already hanging out with Huy and Jens, two of his Shade Brigade buddies who had also decided to splurge. The three of them were watching a soccer game.

Simon and I met Traycee and Karole the next morning during the buffet breakfast. They were costume designers living in Hollywood, California, best friends who worked in the entertainment industry. Karole had a sharp wit and a cheerful disposition, but Traycee was the boss. She about 40 with kinky hair and brown eyes. She was either Mexican American or Puerto Rican. She was a busy woman with a drive to succeed in life, and right now she was up to her eyeballs working in a fast-paced and demanding industry. They were working on a TV series called "Big Brother." Traycee talked and laughed almost too loudly, but then again, I had never met anyone associated with the entertainment industry before.

The breakfast was a colorful buffet with trays of eggs, red and green bell peppers sautéed with onion, a variety of fresh fruit, sausages, golden brown pancakes, waffles made to order, home-fried potatoes, all kinds of juice, and really good coffee. It was a feast! Simon and I stashed some of the pastries and fresh fruit away for later.

We enjoyed engaging conversation with Karole and Traycee. We talked about people we had met on the Camino, places we stayed, and how nice it was to have a full-sized plush white cotton towel. Traycee was trying to figure out how to take the complimentary bathrobe home, but she didn't want to carry it.

After breakfast, I walked through the quiet alleys of León, marveling at the cobblestone streets and architecture of the old buildings. The air was fresh and crisp, the sky clear blue. My feet were still raw and painful, but I had gotten used to them. I still changed out my bandages every morning and took 600mg of ibuprofen when I had to, to reduce the swelling.

THE PATH TAKEN

It seems I have not yet told you about the bright yellow arrows along the Camino. If you are in doubt about being on the right path, look for the yellow arrows. If they do not appear at regular intervals, you need to backtrack until you see them again. They are everywhere along the path and reassure travelers that they have not strayed.

I heard a story about the arrows from a man named Sergio, a big, burly man with a full gray beard and long, matted hair. He was the owner of a roadside café and souvenir shop on the outskirts of Burgos. He wore a large animal-skin coat that could have been llama. His clothing was simple and garnished with a huge black belt and brass belt buckle. He explained that the arrows were a recent addition to the Camino. Back in the early 1970s, a young Spanish priest named Don Elias Valiña Sampedro was assigned to the village of O Cebreiro. He arrived to find the town deserted, except for a few local dairy farmers and two nuns from the Order of Mary. The nuns were long-time hospitaleras for pilgrims.

The priest settled into life in the village. One day he met some pilgrims on the way to Santiago de Compostela. The pilgrims told him they kept getting lost.

Father Elias wanted to find a way to mark the path and decided to walk the Camino the next spring. He, too, got lost several times. As he wandered through León, he found a can of yellow paint that someone had left on the street. That's when Father Elias had his epiphany—the yellow arrows. The paint would be visible and durable.

Painting the arrows became Father Elias's mission. One legend tells of the priest being stopped by the police (Guardia Civil). When they asked him why he was painting yellow arrows all over the place, he said he was preparing for an invasion. The police asked who was going to invade. The humble priest responded that people from all over the world were coming to seek answers to life's mysteries. The police officers pitched in to help. They understood the priest's reason for painting the arrows. Many others followed,

Then the invasion began. Before 1986, fewer than five thousand Compostela were issued each year compared to 276,000 in 2016. Today there are somewhere around 35,000 yellow arrows guiding pilgrims down the ancient trail to the city of Santiago de Compostela and Cape Finisterre.

Sergio, the owner of the café on the outskirts of Burgos, told me this story: Back in the early 1990s when he was a teen, he and several of his friends broke into the Ministry of Transportation maintenance office and stole some yellow paint to give anonymously to Father Elias. Using a borrowed truck, they loaded 500 gallons of bright yellow paint and 40 four-inch paintbrushes from an unlocked warehouse. They set the paint and brushes in the middle of the town square with a note that read, "For the good of the church." The police investigation led right to Father Elias, the mad priest of O Cebreiro. With great effort, Father Elias convinced the police and members of his parish that the paint was indeed a gift from God and for the good of the church, and that it saved the church from buying yellow paint. Many people in the village thought the priest was completely mad. At one point, Father Elias tried to give the paint back, but the Minister of Transportation closed the investigation, not wanting to face political blowback. It was, after all, "for the good of the church." No one was ever arrested for the theft. Sergio claimed to have personally painted thousands of arrows, many more than once. In early spring, he goes to visit old friends and refresh the paint on "his" arrows.

ELEVEN

A HIGHER PLACE

On day 21 we entered the foothills of Galicia. The terrain was dramatically steeper. The Brierley guidebook describes this area as having the steepest incline of the entire Camino.

Simon and I walked together for several days. My routine was to wake early and walk in the cool of the morning to cover some distance. One particular morning, I witnessed the most amazing sunrise in my whole life. It was cool, perhaps in the upper 40s, and a soft white mist in the shallow valley was magically shifting with the gentle breeze. As the sun skirted the eastern horizon, the sky was filled with vibrant purple and orange, soft pink, and wisps of gray. I stopped to witness the brushstrokes of God bringing light to the world. It was a surreal feeling that was exciting, awe-inspiring, and humbling all at the same time.

Once you enter into the third phase of the Camino, your eyes open to the depths of your spirituality. Your soul is affected. This phase is for spiritual mending, and it is shared with the realization that you are going be able to complete the journey. The realization sneaks up on you. Physically, you are in good shape by now. You have just walked 550 kilometers with about 320 more to go. Blisters are healing and you become part of the routine of the Camino. The lesson I learned in the first part of the Camino was to take care of your feet. This part teaches you to take care of your head.

Sometimes I looked at the Camino from a capitalist perspective. I realized that it has been a tourist boon for over a thousand years. The albergues, pensions, and bars are a way of life for people who live along the Camino. Day in and day out, hospitaleros and merchants meet pilgrim after pilgrim.

In a small village just before we reached the Cruz de Ferro were some old, vacant cobblestone two-story buildings from the 1400s. I guess some enterprising family or co-op of residents might have constructed the building as an albergue. Perhaps it was the talk of the region at the time, providing a luxury stay for pilgrims. It might have been like the Parador de León, offering bread, stew, red wine, a warm place to sleep, and maybe even some privacy. I wondered how much they had charged for a simple meal at the end of the day and a cot in a dorm room with a fireplace. Perhaps €8 to €10 would have covered it. Was this even the norm? Or did the typical pilgrim sleep outside wrapped in their cloak? It's unlikely that they had a sleeping pad or a tent. Most pilgrims during medieval times wore long cloaks or wraps. In fact, according to rules enforced by clergy during the 1300s, a pilgrim need to have a cloak in order to be clearly identified. Today your Credencial de Peregrino is your ticket to a reduced room cost and the pilgrim's menu.

As I entered the third phase of my Camino, I met a colorful individual named Roland Meitner. Roland was born and raised in Hanover, Germany, and he taught French to high school students. We discussed religion over a few beers. Roland told me he was an atheist, that he had no belief in God and didn't follow any organized religion. When I asked why he was walking the Camino if he didn't have a spiritual purpose, he could not give me one reason. He had just decided it was time. So when the school term ended, he packed his knapsack, took some money out of the bank, took a few trains to St. Jean Pied-de-Port, and started walking.

In my experience, the beginning of a pilgrimage starts the first time you say to yourself that you are going on a pilgrimage. Then planning takes over your world to the exclusion of everything else. The next thing you know, you are out the door and on the way. Roland and I had many good talks. Was he truly no more than an atheist out for a long walk? I argued that perhaps the spirit of St. James had drawn Roland to the Santiago de Compostela. I assured him he would come to understand the purpose of his Camino, but I could not tell him why I thought so. He alone would learn the truth and wisdom from this journey, and it would change his outlook. I admitted that I was still in deep contemplation on why I was drawn to the Camino.

My conversations with Roland helped me realize that I am a good person and I have a lot to offer this world we live in. How and what I contribute manifests in unexpected ways. I believe in the power of God, that he alone can save me. I surely can't save myself. I believe we all have some belief in a power greater than ourselves. It does not have to be part of an organized religion, but religion makes it easier for me to understand.

No matter my pace in the morning, Simon always caught up by around 10:00 a.m. and we took a break together. He always startled me when he came up from behind, saying, "Hey, Dad." Then my heart would leap, leaving me with a warmth inside, a caring joy that perhaps only a proud father can feel. As we rested one day, I watched Simon, wondering what his life would be like, what pains he would endure, and what joys he would relish.

I reflected on my Camino as I neared the end.

HECTOR RODRIGUEZ

I recalled Matthew, the German soldier I talked about at the very beginning of this story. His experience in battle left him with horrible emotional and visible physical scars. He found peace in walking and finding time to think. And I thought about Todd, the bullfighter, the warrior; Bruno and Silvia, the warrior in love with his bride; and my son, Simon, at the doorstep to manhood.

TWELVE

SANTIAGO DE COMPOSTELA

How does one end a story that will impact the rest of one's life? It is difficult to explain how beliefs are stretched, morphed, and shaped into a single focus. I have met people during my life who seem to have figured out what life is and how religion, politics, humanity, love, and family fit together. It's not that easy for me, and I suspect many people avoid thinking about the hard things in life altogether. It's certainly not easy to evaluate one's meaning and purpose.

A hedonist is someone who lives only for the pursuit of pleasure. What do we call those who find purpose by contributing to the good of humanity, such as someone who studies medicine in order to reduce or eliminate disease or someone who fights poverty? What about the artist who creates a song that touches our spirit or an artist who illuminates passion through colors of paint or sculpting marble? When I arrived in Santiago de Compostela and entered the plaza of the cathedral that holds the relics of St. James, I realized my walk was not ending but rather beginning. Perhaps that is the irony of seeking insight into one's life: the more one seeks, the more one finds to understand. It is a mean trick.

Simon and I entered the Praza do Obradoiro together along with hundreds of other pilgrims. We had met and walked with many, but dozens of pilgrims we had never met were in the square. We put down our packs on the cobblestone plaza and marveled at our surroundings. We had made it to Santiago de Compostela. To the west was the royal Pazo de Raxoi (bishop's palace); to the north was the grand Hostal dos Reis Catolicos Prador hotel; to the south was Colexio de San Xerome, four buildings holding ancient archives that document the history of the Catholic church in Spain; and to the east was the imposing cathedral of St. James. The façade of the cathedral was screened with scaffolding as laborers worked to repair the damage done by water seepage, settling ground, humidity, and automobile exhaust. The preservation efforts were expected to be completed in 2018. At the top center portico of the cathedral stands a statue of St. James. Because the front door was closed as part of the restoration, doors on the east side of the cathedral were opened for access. Known as the Holy Doors, they are normally only opened on years when the Feast of St. James, July 25, falls on a Sunday.

THE PATH TAKEN

The soul of Santiago is the majestic cathedral with its symmetrical spires and sculptures soaring high above the city. The surrounding city grew up around it over several centuries, and the buildings are a mix of Romanesque, Gothic, and baroque architecture. The interior of the cathedral is laid out in the traditional floorplan: a Latin cross with three naves isolated by Romanesque arches. The western facade was constructed in the baroque style in the early 18th century after weather damaged the original Romanesque façade. The façade facing south is the original one built by the Romans. The renowned Pórtico da Gloria is inside the western façade. As one enters the Pórtico da Gloria, over 200 sculptures by Maestro Mateo, the chief designer and builder of the basilica, gaze upon the arriving pilgrims. A statue of the Christ looks out from behind the altar; he is surrounded by angels and the four evangelists. Seated around the throne of Christ are 24 musicians as described in the Book of Revelations. St. James sits at Christ's feet, and below St. James, Hercules holds open the mouths of two lions.

Pilgrims are met with various traditions as they enter the holy Church. At the foot of the statue of St. James, five finger holes have been worn into the marble where countless pilgrims have placed their hand as they entered the massive church. This is where the pilgrim greets St. James for the first time. A pilgrim might bump the head of the sculpture of Maestro Mateo in order to acquire some of his genius. After countless knocks to the head, his smooth face is flat and discolored.

A sculpture of Daniel from the Old Testament prophet shows him with a large smile on his broad face, supposedly in response to the provocatively dressed Queen Esther on an opposite pillar. According to legend, Esther's sculpted breasts were originally much larger, but they were filed down on the orders of a disapproving bishop. In retaliation, the people of Santiago created a cone-shaped *tetilla* (nipple) cheese to honor her. The soft buttery cheese is matured over 10 to 30 days in the hot, humid climate of Galicia. It is thick and smooth with a few holes from pockets of air. I did not have the opportunity to sample it.

The main alter rises majestically at the east end of the cathedral. It is lavishly decorated with marble pillars and gold-inlaid adornments. Wooden hand-carved confessionals line the aisles of the central nave. Each confessional has a list of languages that can be understood at that particular location. Pilgrims are encouraged to attend confession so as to be free of guilt and sin upon arrival. The central nave is filled with heavy wooden pews where visitors may sit or kneel to pray or simply marvel in silence at the ornate construction. At the center of the chancel is the legendary

Botafumeiro, a huge silver censer approximately three feet in diameter and five feet tall. It is used to burn incense during mass. It is swung from a thick rope that runs 300 feet from one end of the transept to the other and is suspended from a swivel-type mechanism attached to the ceiling. The Botafumeiro is only used on certain dates, and it fills the entire cathedral with an earthy, woody fragrance. It was first used during the Middle Ages to cover up the smell of sweaty, unbathed pilgrims.

A downward staircase to the left of the main altar is marked by a brass sign identifying the tomb of St. James: SEPULCRUM SANCTI IACOBI GLORIOSUM. For many pilgrims, it is the final destination of their Camino de Santiago. The remains of a man who knew Jesus Christ rest in a hammered silver box that is 24 inches wide, 36 inches long, 24 inches high. A bouquet of fresh flowers is brought in daily.

Walking the Camino de Santiago was for me a powerful engine for change brought about by contemplation and deep thought. When you take the time to think about your life and are immersed in self-reflection, you look at others differently as well. I found so much humanity along the Camino de Santiago. The adventure instilled hope in me, a hope that we will continue to thrive spiritually and better serve each other.

HECTOR RODRIGUEZ

What have I learned from my Camino experience? It is difficult to say or explain in these few pages. It will take time to better understand the experience and how it will manifest as I enter the fall of my life. I am grateful that my son made the journey with me. I would travel with him anywhere. He is a reasonable, careful, and strong young man. We traveled to the ends of the earth and back together, and I thank him from the bottom of my heart.

ABOUT THE AUTHOR

Hector Rodriguez is originally from San Antonio, Texas. He retired from federal service in 2016 after 30 years. He now lives in Corvallis, Oregon, with his wife and Marco the cat. He enjoys hiking, biking, camping, and other outdoor activities. He is a member of the Scouts of America, the Corvallis Community Writing Group, and the Alliance of Independent Authors.

www.ingramcontent.com/pod-product-compliance
Lightning Source LLC
Chambersburg PA
CBHW071003080526
44587CB00015B/2322